The Global Benefits of Open Research

The 2018 MDPI Writing Prize

The MDPI Writing Prize Series
Volume 1

SERIES EDITOR
Martyn Rittman

The MDPI writing prize aims to promote excellence in scientific writing and explore themes relevant to early career researchers. The inaugural edition took place in 2018 and saw over 40 entries from across the globe. All participants are given the option to publish their entry in an open access book.

Martyn Rittman (Ed.)

The Global Benefits of Open Research

The 2018 MDPI Writing Prize

MDPI • Basel • Beijing • Wuhan • Barcelona • Belgrade

MDPI

SERIES EDITOR
Martyn Rittman
MDPI
Basel, Switzerland

EDITORIAL OFFICE
MDPI
St. Alban-Anlage 66
4052 Basel, Switzerland

For citation purposes, cite each chapter independently as indicated below:

LastName, A.A.; LastName, B.B.; LastName, C.C. Chapter Title. In *The Global Benefits of Open Research. The 2018 MDPI Writing Prize*; Martyn Rittman, Ed., The MDPI Writing Prize Series, Martyn Rittman, Ed.; MDPI: Basel, Switzerland, 2018; Volume 1, Page Range.

VOLUME 1
ISBN 978-3-03897-009-5 (PBK)   ISSN 2624-9693 (Print)
ISBN 978-3-03897-010-1 (PDF)   ISSN 2624-8115 (Online)

Cover image courtesy of MDPI.

Contents

List of Contributors   ix

About the Series Editor   xi

Preface to "The Global Benefits of Open Research"   xiii

1 Addressing Climate Change Through Indigenous Knowledge Systems   1
   Edmond Sanganyado

2 Democratization of Access   4
   Kamala T. Rajagopal

3 Open Scientific Research Is Imperative in the World of the Future   7
   Zhixuan Yin

4 A Futuristic Report on the Global Benefits of Open Research   10
   Daniel Efurosibina Attoye

5 Benefits of Open Research: My Own Stories   13
   Ankur Sarker

6 Open Research as a Tool for Knowledge That Benefits Everyone   16
   Alexandra-Cristina Ticea

7 Commodity or Public Property?   19
   Nils A. Nilsson

8 A Case for Unfettered Access   21
   Ijeoma Priscilla Ugwuanyi

9 The Open Science Revolution   24
   Alessandro Chiadò

10 Open Research—A Supreme Way to Celebrate Your Work   27
   Gagandeep Kaur

11 The Past, Present and Future of Open Access   30
   Syed Shan-e-Ali Zaidi

12 Open Research: Past, Present, and Future   33
   Márió Gajdács

13 Taking the Leap: The Benefits of Open Science   36
   Simon Morand-Beaulieu

14 A Free Piece of Cake   39
   Gianluca Cidonio

15 A Spec of Research to Which Anyone Can Add   42
   Rebecca von Hellfeld

16 The 3 Cs of Open Research: Canalization, Communication and Collaboration   46
   José Jaramillo Ortiz

17 Open Research: A Gateway to Scientific Outreach and Innovation   48
Abel Abera Negash

18 Open Access and Traditional Journal Publications Assessment   50
Pedram Asef

19 Science Should Not Be Kept Behind Paywalls   54
Stefan Stošić

20 Open Research: A Transformative Way Towards Collaboration, Sharing and Dissemination
of Knowledge   57
Lipi Chhaya

21 The Impact of Traditional vs Open Access on Scientific Publications   61
Miquésias Lopes-Pacheco

22 Open Access Research: Bridging the Gap Towards Global Research Improvement   63
Jenichi Clairvaux Felizco

23 The Effects of Open Research on the Scientific World   66
Afrina Mustari

24 Open Sesame!   69
Magaret Sivapragasam

25 The Global Benefits of Open Research and How It Can Change Scientific Publishing   71
Bernhard C. Geiger

26 The Academic, Industrial and Societal Impacts of Open Research   74
Fitya Syarifa Mozar

27 Global Consequences of Open Research   77
Ravi Sahu and Manisha Hariram

28 Drawing an Accessible Future for New Generations   80
Michael Nones

29 The Impact of Open Access on Global Challenges Research   82
Paula Fraga-Lamas

30 Why Care About the Higgs Boson   85
Spiros Kitsinelis

31 Open Research: What's More?   87
Stefano Cinti

32 Open Research: Much Ado About Nothing?   89
Tochukwu Ozulumba

33 Open Research is a Blessing   92
Mai Sabry Saleh

34 Prospects of Global Open Research   95
Auriol Degbelo

35 Open Access: a Two-Way Path for the Underprivileged   99
Stefania Noerman

36 Open Research: Interlinking Sanctuaries of Knowledge   102
James Guo Sheng Moo

List of Contributors

ASEF, PEDRAM. Department of Electrical Engineering, Universitat Politècnica de Catalunya-BarcelonaTech; Barcelona, Spain; pedram.asef@upc.edu.

ATTOYE, DANIEL EFUROSIBINA. Department of Architectural Engineering, College of Engineering, United Arab Emirates University; Al Ain, United Arab Emirates; 201590088@uaeu.ac.ae.

CHHAYA, LIPI. Department of Electronics and Instrumentation Engineering; University of Petroleum and Energy Studies; Dehradun, India; lipi.chhaya@gmail.com.

CHIADÒ, ALESSANDRO. Department of Applied Science and Technology, Politecnico di Torino; Torino, Italy; alessandro.chiado@polito.it.

CIDONIO, GIANLUCA. Faculty of Medicine, University of Southampton; Southhampton, United Kingdom; g.cidonio@soton.ac.uk.

CINTI, STEFANO. Department of Chemical Science and Technologies, University of Rome Tor Vergata; Rome, Italy; stefano.cinti@uniroma2.it.

DEGBELO, AURIOL. Institute for Geoinformatics, University of Münster; Münster, Germany; degbelo@uni-muenster.de.

FELIZCO, JENICHI CLAIRVAUX. Graduate School of Materials Science, Nara Institute of Science and Technology; Nara, Japan; jenichi.felizco.jz1@ms.naist.jp.

FRAGA-LAMAS, PAULA. Department of Computer Engineering; University of A Coruña; A Coruña, Spain; paula.fraga@udc.es.

GAJDÁCS, MÁRIÓ. Institute of Clinical Microbiology, University of Szeged; Szeged, Hungary; gajdacs.mario@med.u-szeged.hu.

GEIGER, BERNHARD. Signal Processing and Speech Communication Laboratory, Graz University of Technology; Graz, Austria; Know-Center GmbH; Graz, Austria; geiger@ieee.org.

HARIRAM, MANISHA. Department of Environmental Science and Engineering, Indian School of Mines, Indian Institute of Technology Dhanbad; Dhanbad, India; mnshaverma10@gmail.com.

KAUR, GAGANDEEP. School of Mathematics, Thapar Institute of Engineering and Technology; Patiala, India; gkaur2@phd16@thapar.edu.

KITSINELIS, SPIROS. Association of Greek Chemists; Athens, Greece; chemchro@eex.gr; kitsinelis@yahoo.gr.

LOPES-PACHECO, MIQUÉIAS. Biosystems and Integrative Sciences Institute (BioISI), University of Lisbon; Lisbon, Portugal; mlopes0811@gmail.com.

MOO, JAMES GUO SHENG. Residues and Resource Reclamation Centre (R3C), Nanyang Environment and Water Research Institute (NEWRI), Nanyang Technological University; Singapore, Singapore; moog0001@e.ntu.edu.sg.

MORAND-BEAULIEU, SIMON. Département de Neurosciences, Université de Montréal; Montréal, Canada; simon.morand-beaulieu@umontreal.ca.

MOZAR, FITYA SYARIFA. Department of Pharmacology, Case Western Reserve University; Cleveland, USA; fsm11@case.edu.

MUSTARI, AFRINA. Department of Physiology, Faculty of Veterinary Science, Bangladesh Agricultural University; Mymensingh, Bangladesh; afrina.mustari@bau.edu.bd.

NEGASH, ABEL ABERA. Armauer Hansen Research Institute; Addis Ababa, Ethiopia; abelishasweet@yahoo.com.

NILSSON, NILS A. Department for Fundamental Research, National Centre for Nuclear Research; Warsaw, Poland; albin.nilsson@ncbj.gov.pl.

NOERMAN, STEFANIA. Department of Clinical Nutrition, Faculty of Health Sciences, University of Eastern Finland; Kuopio, Finland; stefania.noerman@uef.fi.

NONES, MICHAEL. Hydrology and Hydrodynamics Department, Institute of Geophysics, Polish Academy of Sciences; Warsaw, Poland; mnones@igf.edu.pl.

ORTIZ, JOSÉ MANUEL JARAMILLO. Instituto Nacional de Tecnología Agropecuaria (INTA); Buenos Aires, Argentina; pepuspepii@gmail.com.

OZULUMBA, TOCHUKWU. Department of Pharmacy and Biomolecular Sciences, University of Brighton; Brighton, United Kingdom; t.ozulumba@brighton.ac.uk.

RAJAGOPAL, KAMALA T. Asia e University; Subang Jaya, Kuala Lumpur, Malaysia; patriciapauline4321@gmail.com.

SAHU, RAVI. Department of Civil Engineering, Indian Institute of Technology Kanpur; Kanpur, India; ravisahu@iitk.ac.in.

SALEH, MAI SABRY. Environmental and Occupational Medicine Department, Environmental Research Division, National Research Centre; Dokki, Giza, Egypt; nouranomer@gmail.com.

SANGANYADO, EDMOND. Marine Biology Institute, Shantou University; Shantou, China; esang001@ucr.edu.

SARKER, ANKUR. Department of Computer Science University of Virginia; Charlottesville, USA; as4mz@virginia.edu.

SIVAPRAGASAM, MAGARET. Centre of Research in Ionic Liquids (CORIL), PETRONAS University of Technology; Seri Iskandar, Perak Malaysia; magaret.sivapragasam@utp.edu.my; magaret@62@yahoo.co.uk.

STOŠIĆ, STEFAN. Department for Algology, Mycology and Lichenology, Institute of Botany and Botanical Garden "Jevremovac", Faculty of Biology, University of Belgrade / Department for Plant Diseases, Institute for Plant Protection and Environment; Belgrade, Serbia; stefan.stosic@gmail.com.

TICEA, ALEXANDRA. Department of General and Inorganic Chemistry, Faculty of Pharmacy, Carol Davila University of Medicine and Pharmacy; Bucharest, Romania; alexandra.ticea@umfcd.ro.

UGWUANYI, IJEOMA PRISCILLA. Department of Management, College of Business, City University of Hong Kong; Hong Kong, S.A.R China; pugwuanyi2-c@my.cityu.edu.hk.

VON HELLFELD, REBECCA. Centre for Organismal Studies, AG Aquatox, University of Heidelberg; Heidelberg, Germany; rebecca.hellfeld@uni-heidelberg.de.

ZAIDI, SYED SHAN-E-ALI. Plant Genetics Lab, Gembloux Agro-Bio Tech, University of Liège; Liège, Belgium; shan.e.ali@outlook.com.

ZHIXUAN, YIN. College of Environmental and Municipal Engineering; Qingdao University of Technology; Qingdao, China; yinzhixuan@qut.edu.cn.

About the Series Editor

MARTYN RITTMAN received his PhD in 2008 from the University of Warwick, UK followed by postdoctoral positions at the University of Reading, UK and the University of Freiburg, Germany. He joined MDPI as an editor in 2013. As Publishing Services Manager Dr. Rittman oversees several projects, including the English editing department and the interdisciplinary preprint server hosted at Preprints.org.

Preface to "The Global Benefits of Open Research"

This book is the result of the 2018 MDPI Writing Prize, in which entrants were asked to write up to 1000 words on the topic of "The global benefits of open research". Beyond that, no guidance was given in terms of format or style, and some of the entries show a particularly unique approach to the topic. It is a collection of diverse, thought-provoking, and visionary ideas. I congratulate all of the authors on their contribution and the time and effort they put into writing the short essays it contains. A few common themes were evident, including benefits to the following:

- researchers in general;
- researchers in the global south;
- wider society;
- the economy of countries operating open science policies.

Another feature was a strong focus on open access, sometimes to the point of using open access and open research interchangeably. Perhaps this is a signal that open access has become well established, whereas other forms of open research require further development.

The winning entries are presented first, followed by entries group roughly into the topics above, although several essays mention multiple aspects. The competition was only open to those whose first language is not English and only minor language editing has taken place between submission and publication. Grammatical errors have been removed, but the original phrasing was retained where possible. As such, the ideas of these young researchers are presented in an unfiltered way that reflects their own choice of words, style of writing, and in particular their thoughts and emotions about the topic.

Much effort was obviously undertaken to research the essays presented here, however thorough fact-checking has not taken place and minor errors and misunderstandings may remain. While not intending to mislead, I believe the value of this book lies principally in the enthusiasm and vision of the essays, not as a reference work. I take responsibility for this editorial decision and errors should in no way detract from the efforts of the authors.

Finally, this book is published in an open access format and free to download and read. It may also be reused and quoted from. I hope readers will find the perspectives presented here useful and take advantage of the opportunity to reflect on how open research can develop for the benefit of all.

Martyn Rittman
Series Editor

1 Addressing Climate Change through Indigenous Knowledge Systems

Edmond Sanganyado

Hiding from the blistering heat, a brawny calf with a short papyrus rope tied around its neck leaned on a mopane tree. Tears rolled down the calf's eyes as if aware of its impending doom. A swarm of flies delivered a sad eulogy as they buzzed around the calf's nose. An uninvited cloud of dust swirled at a distant driven by the hot and dry winds. It was almost Christmas time, yet the clouds were empty, the rivers had dried, the grass was all gone, and the cattle were dying. Any hope of survival was fast disappearing like morning dew on a sunny summer morning.

In high school, we were taught that the southern parts of Zimbabwe, particularly in the Beitbridge district, were only suitable for animal husbandry rather than crop cultivation. Eager to know why, I visited a local library and delved into several geography textbooks. Land degradation was turning parts of the Beitbridge district into a desert. Perennial erratic rainfalls made the district susceptible to droughts. In the past two decades, the frequency of droughts has significantly increased, possibly due to climate change [1]. The calf was the latest victim of climate change after losing its mother at birth.

Storytelling as Open Research

"It is the cycle of life", one villager said, fruitlessly trying to conceal the pain of losing a dozen cattle due to lack of water in the once majestic Mzingwane River and its tributaries. "Our loss is a gain to the forests because when cattle die, they decompose into valuable nutrients essential for plant growth". The explanation was startling considering a cow is a symbol of wealth among the Venda people in Beitbridge. My brother-in-law once told me a story of a Venda village in Beitbridge where the community rejected plans to build a school. The village elders argued the school would take away important grazing land for their cattle. It is quite unfortunate that the government officials from the ministry of education probably dismissed the perceptions of the villagers and labeled them primitive, pedestrian, and unproductive.

Although despicable, researchers often view themselves as the saviors imbued with unassailable scientific wisdom to address global challenges [2]. Listening to the villagers talk about the loss of cattle, short and erratic rain seasons, increased atmospheric temperatures, and a decrease in wild fruits, I realized they understood climate change probably better than most climate experts. Without using scientific jargon or citing the latest climate science research, the villagers discussed the causes, effects, and possible adaptation and mitigation strategies using folklore, proverbs, and personal observations. The villagers were not hopeless, ignorant, and primitive victims as portrayed in many academic studies and media reports. What fascinated me was that the villagers openly shared their knowledge, experience, and observation. They allowed fellow villagers to critique their views publicly. Theories about climate change were proposed, rebuffed or supported openly. The villagers were knowledgeable experts who required collaborations rather than consultations with the government and climate scientists.

Openness in Indigenous Knowledge Systems

In many African communities, knowledge is not an attribute of an individual, but is collectively owned by the community. Indigenous knowledge systems have survived for many centuries without preservation as written text. Personal observations are often celebrated as a key resource for the acquisition of new knowledge. This is best illustrated by Shona proverbs such as *afamba apota*—traveler sees what lies beyond sight—and *takabva neko, kumhunga hakuna ipwa*—we have been there, there are no sweet sorghums in a millet farm. Together with proverbs and folklore, personal observations knitted into stories are shared openly during social gatherings such as funerals, weddings, community harvests, or religious meetings. Thus, in many African communities, storytelling is the academic research equivalent to open data. Listeners are free to use the story in any way meaningful to their contexts. Hence, openness is the key ingredient for knowledge preservation and transmission in indigenous knowledge systems, particularly in Zimbabwean communities [3].

Recently, I searched for articles on climate change in Africa using SCOPUS and found around 27,840 documents. However, less than 7% of the documents were available through open access. Hiding research behind paywalls does a great disservice to the communities that funded the research or took part in the research as subjects. The scientific community should learn about the importance of openness from indigenous knowledge systems. For example, through living in proximity to the environment, indigenous people developed a knowledge system important in climate science. The indigenous knowledge is openly policed through taboos, preserved through folklore and proverbs, and transmitted through storytelling [2,4]. Researchers have taken advantage of the openness in indigenous knowledge and used it to compliment climate science in areas where meteorological data is absent [1,5]. Indigenous people did not hide their personal observations behind subscriptions; they freely share with researchers, thus contributing to the advancement of climate science.

References

1. Chivenge, P.; Mabhaudhi, T.; Modi, A.T.; Mafongoya, P. The potential role of neglected and underutilised crop species as future crops under water scarce conditions in Sub-Saharan Africa. *Int. J. Environ. Res. Public Health* **2015**, *12*, 5685–5711. [CrossRef] [PubMed]
2. Maldonado, J.; Bennett, T.M.B.; Chief, K.; Cochran, P.; Cozzetto, K.; Gough, B.; Redsteer, M.H.; Lynn, K.; Maynard, N.; Voggesser, G. Engagement with indigenous peoples and honoring traditional knowledge systems. *Clim. Chang.* **2016**, *135*, 111–126. [CrossRef]
3. Sanganyado, E.; Teta, C.; Masiri, B. Impact of African traditional worldviews on climate change adaptation. *Integr. Environ. Assess. Manag.* **2018**, *14*, 189–193. [CrossRef] [PubMed]
4. Zuma-Netshiukhwi, G.; Stigter, K.; Walker, S. Use of traditional weather/climate knowledge by farmers in the South-Western free State of South Africa: Agrometeorological learning by scientists. *Atmosphere (Basel)* **2013**, *4*, 383–410. [CrossRef]
5. Soropa, G.; Gwatibaya, S.; Musiyiwa, K.; Rusere, F.; Mavima, G.A.; Kasasa, P. Indigenous knowledge system weather forecasts as a climate change adaptation strategy in smallholder farming systems of Zimbabwe: Case study of Murehwa, Tsholotsho and Chiredzi districts. *Afr. J. Agric. Res.* **2015**, *10*, 1067–1075. [CrossRef]

2 Democratization of Access

Kamala T. Rajagopal

At 10:56 p.m. on 20 July 1969, a "giant leap for mankind" was made by Neil Armstrong. He stepped on the moon from the lunar ensemble 'Eagle', an astronaut of the first manned flight of the Saturn V rocket. He left behind an American flag and a plaque. It read "Here man from the planet earth, first set foot upon the moon. We come in peace for all mankind". Half a billion people watched the awe-inspiring achievement on television.

We have made stupendous leaps in knowledge from that spectacular moment to this present time. Knowledge breakthroughs have occurred not only in outer space but on earth as well. MIT's tiny roboclam digs underwater seabeds to implant anchors for giant ocean liners [1]. Tesla has produced the world's first ever premium all electric sedan [2] and Airbus' flying car Vahana made its maiden flight just recently in Oregon [3].

So what is the difference between our past moments of glory and the present times? It is in the amazing levels at which knowledge grows and is disseminated through the world wide web. It took about a hundred years from the first tentative telescopic photographing of the moon to the actual landing. But the last ten years of this millenium have been crowded with similar landings on Titan (2005), the giant asteroid Vesta (2011) and the dwarf planet Ceres (2015). A consumer car, the Falcon Cherry [4], has been sent to space this very year. This knowledge revolution has gone hand in hand with a phenomenal rate of knowledge dissemination, and a special internet version of it called 'open publishing' has taken the world by storm.

This relatively new idea means research data is offered freely to the public to download, disseminate or use without legal, financial and technical restrictions. It is undertaken through journals, e-books and dissertations. Open access has turned the world on its head, with the number of journals offering open access almost doubling from 2000 to 4400 in just two years [5]. The shift from commercial to academic and individual initiatives in the publishing field means that a lone researcher in a shack somewhere in the third world could access a wide range of international data on everything from global warming to AIDS research. Old knowledge can be reinvented and new insights obtained. Intellectual borders could be crossed at high speed with less of the friction paying research entails. Scholars in metadata harvesting and interdisciplinary research could benefit greatly from open access portals. Scholarly institutions practicing the 'open' paradigm can heighten their profiles, save on internal expense and create brand awareness for themselves and their members.

But what exactly is the greatest benefit of open publications? Personally for me, it is the democratic access and the levelling of the playing fields for all that really matters. As Margaret Fuller, the renowned 19th century philosopher aptly said, "If you have knowledge let others light their candles in it." Knowledge therefore is meant to be given and not hoarded. Many in the third world have financial fuel tanks that run on 'empty 'or 'near empty'. As a developing world researcher myself, I am quite familiar with this scenario. My father, with sheer hard work and a meager salary, ran a ten member household, putting five children through university almost simultaneously. The sound of squalling babies and cats rummaging bins was a common scene then and even now, as I access open data on my aged computer. The constraints are certainly there.

So as we run at stellar speed for achievements in outer space or closer to home, we could achieve touchdown I say, through open web access. It could provide a leg up for those who run on 'empty' or 'near empty'. As I peruse ethnographic data (my specialty), accounts of science teaching in remote locations like Bhutan or in the public schools of New York all become a reality. The cool mountain air of Bhutan and the noisy chaos of American high schools are there on my laptop for me to fathom and decipher. There is an understanding, a fellowship and camaraderie, an exchange of communication between faraway participants that would have been near impossible if the financial constraints of closed publishing were firmly in place. There would have been less probing, less depth and scope in my research, less academic connectivity, and less citations for my fellow global scholars.

In summary, I reiterate that open access addresses cultural conditions in scholarly research in fields ranging from space exploration to the more pressing areas of poverty, housing and economic development. It reduces institutional and personal deficits for those who cannot pay for research products on a daily basis. It democratizes intellectual gain. It speeds dissemination of scholarly output by reducing the friction of paid publishing methodologies. The elitist nature of web research, with greater gains for those with greater capital, and less advantages for those with less, will become a thing of the past as open publication concepts catch fire. Therefore, those who endorse and propagate the open access paradigm should be respected for it. In concluding, I quote the fourteenth Dalai Lama of Tibet, "Share your knowledge, it is a way to immortality".

References

1. Thomspon, E.A. Dig This: RoboClam, 2015. MIT News. Available online: http://news.mit.edu/2008/roboclam-1125 (accessed on 10 October 2018).
2. Tesla. Available online: https://www.tesla.com/models (accessed on 10 October 2018).
3. Airbus. Vahana, the Self-Piloted, EVTOL Aircraft From A^3 by Airbus, Successfully Completes Frist Full-Scale Test Flight, 2018. Airbus. Available online: https://www.airbus.com/newsroom/press-releases/en/2018/02/vahana--the-self-piloted--evtol-aircraft-from-a--by-airbus--succ.html (accessed on 10 October 2018).
4. Dunn, M. Space sports car now flying toward asteroid belt beyond Mars, 2018. Phys. Org. Available online: https://phys.org/news/2018-02-space-sports-car-asteroid-belt.html (accessed on 10 October 2018).
5. Björk, B.-C. The Hybrid Model for Open Accss Publication of Scholarly Articles: A Failed Experiment? *J. Am. Soc. Inf. Sci. Tec.* **2012**, *63*, 1496–1504. [CrossRef]

3   Open Scientific Research Is Imperative in the World of the Future

Zhixuan Yin

When I was a child, I was educated to share. However, from the day I entered the academic world, I was not encouraged to share. Locking the work I publish in well-known journals and carrying my experimental data with me, my mentor, my peers and I developed a competitive rather than a cooperative relationship. Every day, we may get amazing discoveries, some of which can even save lives or change the world. However, we lock the information in journals and most people can't read it. After all, in many areas of the world, journal subscription is still too expensive. E-subscription of a high-quality journal may have expenditure equal to the annual salary of a researcher. Hence, research institutions in some countries often have to make choices between hosting research projects, paying researchers, and buying e-journals. The result is often abandoning subscriptions.

The lack of access to information hinders learning, stifles innovation and slows the research process. I have witnessed my colleagues working on public health issues racking their brains about how to get papers on the latest developments in their field. I also saw anxiety from students who wanted to find out more about a new topic only to encounter one payment threshold after another. I also have to deal with these paid pages every day. Eventually, I am able to read some of the authors' articles that I want to track through e-mail or social media. But there are still some articles that I cannot read. And I wonder every day whether I missed a lot of information associated with my research. As a researcher who is still in the early stages of the career, I am committed to making sure that my work can be made public and I have given up publishing in closed access journals. My mentor and some peers told me that this behavior is suicide for my career. But I believe not. After publication, whether it is through open access journals or not, it can bring more comments and suggestions for the work. And this is important especially for inexperienced researchers who are trying hard to let people remember their names.

Over the last decade, a series of academic movements have been initiated aimed at overcoming the drawbacks of traditional scientific research. These movements highlighted the concept of "freedom, openness, cooperation, and sharing". So-called "open scientific research movements" formed a stark contrast with the closure of traditional scientific research. The FOSTER research report mentioned that open scientific research includes open source software, open data, open access, open research methods, open peer review, and open educational resources, etc. [1]. Among them, open access and open data play crucial roles in the open scientific research movement. They allow scientific research to be shared, copied, displayed, and published in a fast and efficient manner. "Because of the ability to share good scientific research results and to spread and exchange knowledge in an unrestricted way, you can increase mutual understanding, encourage each other, and promote healthy competition" said Dr. Ed Gerstner, Head of Open Research, Greater China, Nature Publishing Group [2]. Open access cannot only expand the dissemination ability of traditional academic journal papers, but also be beneficial to the mutual encouragement, cooperation and progress of scientific research in the future. Through data sharing and other people's evaluation and analysis, the sharers can know the credibility of their data and research direction and many "rejected" data can be used. At the same time, sharing data can also help expand the possibility of scientific research cooperation and promote multidisciplinary cooperation, which is also conducive to fulfilling the enormous potential of the scientific research community.

The advent of Science 2.0, preprinting, open peer review, open data repositories, and innovation driven by the socialization of scientific research through the use of internet, promotes the diversification of scientific exchanges and provides a breeding ground for the birth of an open scientific era. The OECD report "Making open science a reality" pointed out that network and online platforms provide new opportunities for the organization and publication of research projects, scientific literature, and large data sets [3]. Information and communication technologies make it possible to collect large-scale data and information as the basis of scientific experiments and research, making science more and more driven by data. And online storage makes it easier to obtain and use scientific research information. All these have accelerated the transfer of knowledge between researchers and fields, opened up new ways of cooperation and new research methods, and led to the rapid development of "open scientific research".

As global scientific and technological cooperation has become increasingly widespread and science and technology innovation organizations in different countries have infiltrated each other, open scientific research is becoming a national strategy. The "Open Science and Research Roadmap 2014–2017" released by The Finnish Ministry of Education and Culture, clearly stated that Finland should become the leader country of open research in 2017 [4]. Horizon 2020 proposed publicly-funded research in Europe to ensure and strengthen open access to scientific publications and scientific data. A series of reports concerning the "European Union's 7th Framework Programme" issued by the Council of the European Union pointed out that with open scientific research as a link, it constantly expands innovative research and further realizes the ideal state of "Open to the World" [5].

Accompanied by opportunities and challenges, the openness still needs to be broadened to cover every area of scientific research. And open scientific research should not be confined to researchers engaged in scientific work, but involve publishers, enterprise and the entire public worldwide. Moving toward open scientific research brings new interests, new models, new rules, new policies, and new mechanisms emerged in knowledge creation, information dissemination, results sharing, knowledge application, scientific research organization, and performance evaluation. Even though there are still certain problems under discussion in the aspects of policies, intellectual property and information security, open scientific research is imperative in the future world.

References

1. European Commission Community Research and Development Information Service (CORDIS). FOSTER Final Report Summary, 2017. CORDIS EU. Available online: https://cordis.europa.eu/docs/results/612/612425/final1-foster-final-report.pdf (accessed on 10 October 2018).
2. Gerstner, E. From Open Access to Open Research. Finding New Routes to Collaboration and Discovery. Persented at From Open Access to Open Research, National Science Library (Chinese Academy of Sciences) Beinjing, China, 23 September 2014.
3. Organisation for Economic Co-operation and Development (OECD). Making Open Science a Reality, 2015. OECD iLibrary. Available online: https://www.oecd-ilibrary.org/science-and-technology/making-open-science-a-reality_5jrs2f963zs1-en (accessed on 10 October 2018).
4. Ministry of Education and Culture Finland. Open science and research leads to surprising discoveries and creative insights: Open science and research roadmap 2014–2017, 2014. Available online: https://openscience.fi/documents/14273/0/Open+Science+and+Research+Roadmap+2014-2017/e8eb7704-8ea7-48bb-92e6-c6c954d4a2f2 (accessed on 10 October 2018).
5. European Commission Research & Innovation (CORDIS). FP7. Available online: https://ec.europa.eu/research/fp7/index_en.cfm (accessed on 10 October 2018).

4 A Futuristic Report on the Global Benefits of Open Research

Daniel Efurosibina Attoye

According to historical records, there were several precarious situations across the globe at the start of the 21st century. Africa was plagued with the Ebola outbreak, the American continent dealt with severe rainstorms and floods; these were followed by the Middle Eastern Syrian upheavals and the short European Union dichotomy spurred by Brexit. But it was the global environmental and energy crises which plagued the century the most. Australian-born Martin Green and Swiss-born Michael Gratzel drove the research community in solar energy which significantly spurred energy sustainability in that century. At this time, open research was a debate with significant restraining factors such as data validity and web abuse [1], financial support, quality and value of research data [2], cloud storage and data security [3]. However, the resolution of the environmental and energy challenges in the middle of the century spurred a new age of open research collaborations. The path was laid but still needed leadership and harmony on a global scale. Schmidt [1] had noted that travel cost savings and instant feedback allowed the World Wide Web to spur new research opportunities. In 2014, the West African Ebola outbreak was stymied in Nigeria with possibly thousands of lives saved. The Nigerian approach had adopted online research findings from publications like Spengler et al. [4] calling for adequate surveillance, diagnosis and better community understanding about the disease.

Today is January 1, 2120 and open research is no longer a debate; the Juéwàng ("hopeless") Crisis (2116–2120) of the last decade was the rallying point of the World Science Hub (WSH) and is proof of the success of an international collaborative effort. Open research had flourished for over 50 years in the scientific community but an eminent global epidemic had placed the world in danger of an extinction-level event. The Juéwàng Crisis began four years ago when astronomers at the North Atlantic Observatory noticed a small earthbound achondrite meteor. It was later shot down but an encrusted alien pathogenic organism stowed away on the meteor into Earth. It mutated and spawned in the oceans where the fragments had landed; the resulting infections were calamitous. The World Science Hub set up a 4-Phase Emergency Response; firstly, define the core source, next gather relevant data, analyze gathered data and develop mitigation strategies. The American, African and Asian continents were most affected due to the ocean currents at the time; Europe provided humanitarian relief and skilled personnel to the research stations.

In Phase 1, top scientists met online to debate this global challenge, migration of the aquatic pathogenic carrier and reported sightings. High tide, ocean currents, and intercontinental drift made it difficult to define the exact location of the organism. Although the American station reported the most recent sightings, the African station had noticed the most severe outbreak. It was a combination of ocean mapping using undersea stations and miniature marine drones across the three stations that eventually pinpointed the location of the organism in Asia. Economic barriers were swiftly addressed as the global effort released funds for a 1000 km modular seafront barrier set to contain physical movement. The European station installed the ASE 2 (Aquatic Sonic Ell) program developed to protect endangered marine organisms during the last Underwater Olympic Games in 2118. These collaborative scientific, economic and technical efforts were particularly crucial to the success of Phase 1.

Data Collection and Analysis Phases were estimated to take 12 months if run in a single station but only took 4 weeks! It was a global campaign as research institutes, government agencies, and non-governmental organizations deployed advanced ocean mapping satellites, ocean divers, and aquatic drones to gather every piece of data on the epidemic. As the projected 6-month timeline before the pandemic ominously approached, the global effort saved much needed time. But it was the analysis phase that proved more miraculous. The American station connected the Hub to her energy-self-sustaining Moon-orbiting station powered by the prototype Web 7.0. The flow of information and refinement of methodology for various stages of analysis across the Hub was seamless; if it wasn't a crisis situation one would have relished a time of such scientific harmony of intent and display of open research passion.

In the final phase, the WSH met with presidential representatives to develop country-specific solutions to the mutating virus. At this point economic altercations, intellectual property rights, research ownership, and low governmental will had been trounced. The single goal was to save the human race. That represents the aim of open research; regardless of the taunts of critics, the benefits outweigh the challenges. The conclusion of this report drawing from two centuries of research brings to light via a case study approach the opportunities and global benefits of open research.

Daniel Efurosibina Attoye

References

1. Schmidt, W.C. World-Wide Web Survey Research: Benefits, Potential Problems, and Solutions. *Behav. Res. Method., Ins., & Comp.* **1997**, *29*, 274.
2. Sveinsdottir, T.; Wessels, B.A.; Smallwood, R.; Linde, P.; Kala, V.; Tsoukala, V.; Sondervan, J. Policy Recommendations for Open Access to Research Data in Europe—Stakeholder Values and Ecosystems. *Inf. Serv. & Use* **2014**, *34*, 331–333.
3. Hashem, I.A.T.; Yaqoob, I.; Anuar, N.B.; Mokhtar, S.; Gani, A.; Khan, S.U. The Rise of "Big Data" on Cloud Computing: Review and Open Research Issues. *Inf. Syst.* **2015**, *47*, 98–115. [CrossRef]
4. Spengler, J.R.; Ervin, E.D.; Towner, J.S.; Rollin, P.E.; Nichol, S.T. Perspectives on West Africa Ebola Virus Disease Outbreak, 2013–2016. *Emerg. Infect. Dis.* **2016**, *22*, 956. [CrossRef] [PubMed]

5 Benefits of Open Research: My Own Stories

Ankur Sarker

As a Ph.D. student for a few years in the field of computing science, I have come to realize the benefits of making research globally accessible. I come from a small third-world country where most research publications are not available. In my undergraduate university, we were only able to access IEEE Xplore Digital Library [1] in my 4th year of college, and that access was only available until the institution encountered some budget issues and ended its IEEE subscription. Later, when I joined my Ph.D. program in the US, I realized the benefits of having subscriptions of major publication organizations in my field. Researchers in the under-developed world often do not have access to the current and upcoming trends in certain research areas. When any research work is not made openly accessible, its impact both on that country's policy makers and on the wider research community is limited. Most importantly, in the developing world, open research raises the profile of research performed both locally and globally. In my understanding, greater access to global scientific studies and their results can improve the effectiveness of research work in four ways: increase research efficiency, reduce costs by preventing duplicate work, enable the transfer of knowledge and the reuse of datasets to produce more research work, and increase the connectivity among researchers for national and worldwide participation in the research process. In this essay, I am going to share my understanding of the global dividends of open research through some of my personal experiences.

Primarily, the efficiency of a research project is vastly increased if it is open to all other research communities. For instance, one day my Ph.D. supervisor called a meeting with another research group to discuss a tentative collaborative work scenario. Surprisingly, during our discussion, we found that both groups were pursuing the same goal and were using a similar approach. If these works had already been open to all, we could have ended up helping each other and would have avoided repetitive workloads. If the research work is open and well-advertised, any further studies could directly use the open study to extend the topic even further. In this way, any drawbacks of an original work can be diminished and we can also avoid unnecessary repetition. Openly accessible scientific findings and resources (e.g., evaluation procedures, datasets, and so on) offer the opportunities for rigorous evaluations and scrutiny by the scientific community all over the world, which allows a more optimized replication and widely acceptable validation of the research work. In this process, it is easier to find incompetence in research work at a very early stage, and set an example for the scientific community to avoid any scientific misconduct and preserve scientific integrity. In this sense, openness to data helps to maintain science's self-correction principle. In addition, there is a significant increase in citations when the research works are made openly available to more researchers.

In a more connected world, the greater access to scientific innovation offers opportunities to share the risks in future research. First, open innovation can reduce the cost of reproducibility. No researcher would waste time and effort conducting a study if the researcher knows it has already been accomplished. However, duplication of effort is all-too-possible and all-too-probable when researchers cannot effectively communicate with one another and make results known to others in their field and beyond. Second, open research helps to increase the collaboration between different research groups who would together share the risks with the rewards, and this would create more innovation. This approach has realized notable benefits in many areas, including IT, healthcare, public policy, and so on.

Open research and increased access to research results can foster innovation and creativity more broadly. For example, sharing acquired knowledge with others can be useful in making the knowledge more robust, diverse, and applicable in scenarios that are more practical. I like the idea used in the machine learning field called the "transfer learning approach" where researchers use a previously trained machine learning model in different scenarios. In this way, the researchers can skip pre-training the model which costs hours of computation resources. Open research enables re-using the research finding and large-scaled datasets by individuals and research organizations. In most circumstances, openly accessible research promotes a swifter path from idea generation to product development by reducing the delays. In my last research paper, I benefitted by using an open source traffic dataset from an organization. This saved the time I would have needed to collect and pre-process raw data, and it added extra value to my research as the used dataset is very large-scale.

As a student, I certainly realize how open source work can increase the connectivity among researchers and collaborators. Due to the staggering price of journal subscriptions, many well-established institutions cannot always provide their students with the complete scholarly record. Even though I am attending a well-established university, I have found that I do not have access to some publications from some journal publishing organizations that require an especially high subscription rate. I can imagine that students from the smaller or less well-funded universities have to face the challenges to fully utilize the limited access to research work their libraries can afford. I also have found that some of my post-graduate lab mates cannot access some prestigious publications after their graduation while they are working in the university in conjunction with industry. This is a hindrance for their enthusiasm towards research. Open research can globally connect many researchers all over the world and they can share their ideas in achieving a better future for humankind.

From the above discussion, I can simply conclude that the global benefits of open research are not constrained only to the scientific communities or researchers themselves. They also serve to benefit the whole society, including individual citizens and the public and private sectors.

Reference

1. IEEE Xplore Digital Library. Available online: https://ieeexplore.ieee.org/Xplore/home.jsp (accessed on 10 October 2018).

6   Open Research as a Tool for Knowledge That Benefits Everyone

Alexandra-Cristina Ticea

The core idea of open research is the free-of-charge access to research results, methods, software, and also access to fellowships, state-of-the-art research facilities and equipment, open courses etc. The most tangible and prevalent form in which open research is objectified is probably represented by open access (OA) journals.

This subject has attracted extensive attention among the members of the academic and publishing communities, beginning with the release of the free online journal Psycoloquy by Stevan Harnad [1]. The Internet has created tremendous opportunities, has contributed to information apprehension and exchange at a previously unimagined pace. Inherently, this aspect led to the concept of free and facile access to information and knowledge. Indeed, OA journals have constantly grown and improved along with the Internet and as of February 2018, the Directory of Open Access Journals (www.doaj.org) contained a total of 11,169 OA journal titles, belonging to virtually all academic fields.

The favourable evolution of OA publishing comes as a consequence of the fact that it rewards both authors and readers. Most scholars find that the most compelling reason to publish in OA journals is the free accessibility of the articles. This is quite easy to comprehend, since visibility is generally an important factor when deciding which journal to publish in. According to Davis et al., full-text downloads of OA articles are 89% higher, PDF downloads are 42% higher, and the number of unique visitors are 23% higher than those for subscription-based papers [2].

Moreover, a broader readership, increased findability and accessibility most often brings higher citation scores for a certain paper and hence, increased research impact. A parenthesis should however be made here. Citation rate and frequency are mostly increased by these factors for the meritorious articles, which bring relevant and original data to the scientific world [3]. In addition, OA publishing facilitates the transition to new citation metrics, such as the Relative Citation Ratio (RCR) [4] or Citex [5], which quantify the impact of individual articles rather than that of the journal. Since journal impact factors are poorly correlated with actual citations of individual articles, these new citation metrics are generally considered to be more relevant [6].

Another important advantage of publishing in OA journals is the fast publication times. In the era of speed that we live in, faster impact and faster access to information is crucial. The too long publishing cycles in traditional print are obsolete and researchers are able to build on existing research more quickly. For instance, a statistical analysis performed on 2700 papers published in 135 journals listed in the Scopus citation index, showed that the time from acceptance to publication is considerably shorter for OA journals compared to non-OA journals [7].

Furthermore, most OA journals cross multiple disciplines, which leads to increased interdisciplinary conversation, wider research impact and greater visibility. These aspects eventually facilitate concerted research on a global scale, empowered through partnerships between academia, research institutions and other parties. This wider collaboration renders the establishment of extensive research frameworks possible.

OA journals make scientific content available to those who cannot access subscription-based articles, which implies greater public engagement. This aspect may bring in additional views with a positive note on research impact, funding opportunities and practical applications. Open research generates feedback loops, which is the case for every open system. If these feedback loops are properly maintained, they can offer useful insight, fruitful ideas and collaborations.

Over the past few years, open access has been regarded as a solution to the "serials crisis". This crisis refers to the alarmingly increasing number of libraries that have been forced to cut journal subscriptions because of the unreasonably high prices involved for full online access to articles. It is self-evident that scientific results locked behind a paywall render the prospect of any progress limited to the privileged few.

OA journals offer researchers in developing countries and small or specialized research institutions access to the content/knowledge and the possibility of publishing. High impact non-open access journals may be biased against research performed in developing countries or by researchers who are not part of renowned scientific groups. OA journals, however, have a more open policy towards these scholars.

In an ideal society, scientists only concentrate on research, not resources. However, the lack of access to research facilities and state-of-the-art equipment for scientists from developing countries represents another important issue. Opening laboratory doors in highly developed countries, offering support and sharing experience to these researchers will most definitely represent an important boost towards the development of third-world countries' research achievements. This might be, in turn, beneficial to societal development in these regions.

Therefore, there are compelling reasons to encourage open research in a global context. OA can become a tremendous tool of collective empowerment for underdeveloped countries and of on-going accumulation of knowledge through research. Science and society stand to gain much if a sincere commitment is made towards creating and maintaining a real openness to all scientific results for any category of researchers, so that knowledge can easily spread and be built upon. This openness within science will unambiguously generate invaluable results that will bring about a more transparent, open and interactive society.

References

1. Harnad, S. Scholarly skywriting and the prepublication continuum of scientific inquiry. *Psychol. Sci.* **1990**, *1*, 342–343. [CrossRef]
2. Davis, P.M.; Lewenstein, B.V.; Simon, D.H.; Booth, J.G.; Connolly, M.J.L. Open access publishing, article downloads, and citations: Randomised controlled trial. *BMJ* **2008**, *337*, a568. [CrossRef] [PubMed]
3. Xia, J. A longitudinal study of scholars attitudes and behaviors toward open-access journal publishing. *J. Am. Soc. Inf. Sci.* **2010**, *61*, 615–624. [CrossRef]
4. Hutchins, B.I.; Yuan, X.; Anderson, J.M.; Santangelo, G.M. Relative Citation Ratio (RCR): A New Metric That Uses Citation Rates to Measure Influence at the Article Level. *PLoS Biol.* **2016**, *14*, e1002541. [CrossRef] [PubMed]
5. Pal, A.; Ruj, S. CITEX: A new citation index to measure the relative importance of authors and papers in scientific publications. In Proceedings of the 2015 IEEE International Conference on Communications (ICC), London, UK, 8–12 June 2015; pp. 1256–1261.
6. Antelman, K. Do Open-Access Articles Have a Greater Research Impact? *Coll. Res. Libr.* **2004**, *65*, 372–382. [CrossRef]
7. Björk, B.C.; Solomon, D.J. The publishing delay in scholarly peer-reviewed journals. *J. Informetr.* **2013**, *7*, 914–923. [CrossRef]

7 Commodity or Public Property?

Nils A. Nilsson

The first scientific journals which started regularly publishing new ideas and results in an organised way were launched in 1665 in France and the United Kingdom. The idea was that by collecting new science in one place, scientists could save much work and effort by not having to distribute their results in the form of written letters. Moreover, as the journals recorded the exact dates of received material, it became easier to give credit appropriately. Previous to this, it was not always clear who had been the first to arrive at a certain result. Since then, the world has grown smaller, and today there are thousands of peer reviewed academic journals available both online and in print. However, a large fraction of these publications are available only through a subscription, which comes at a steep cost, and individuals outside of academia might feel reluctant to put up the money required for access. Whilst there are preprint servers out there, these are not peer reviewed, and articles published there may contain mistakes and inconsistencies. It is therefore imperative to have access to the publication in its final form, which means needing access to a journal, through a paywall.

An engineering student from Germany, a schoolteacher from Sudan, or a decision maker from Japan, these are people who might want access to the latest research publications, but because of paywalls, will almost certainly have trouble finding what they need. If publications were available free of charge, these people, and many more would have instant access to the very forefront of human knowledge. In fact, the benefits of open access publishing vastly outweigh the drawbacks. Studies have shown that research published in an open access journal receives more reads. In fact, open publications are more likely to receive attention from the public, from news outlets, and perhaps more importantly, from researchers in other fields who tend to not pay for access to a journal which is not in their area of expertise. Open access will help erase these borders and encourage interdisciplinary research and collaboration. There is also the issue of data ownership; it is not unheard of for large corporations and even governments to try to influence the outcome of certain studies and research projects. This would become a lot easier to detect and stop if data and results were open access. As it is now, it is not always clear who owns the data, the university or the scientist? A simple open data repository might help to alleviate this problem, so that the data used to obtain certain results is freely available to everyone.

So why is not all research open access? Unfortunately, there is more than one side to this coin. One of the more pragmatic reasons for paywalls and subscriptions is that running and managing a high-quality scientific journal does not come cheap. Although the vast majority of peer reviewers receive no salary for their work, the editing, proof-reading, and managing web services all cost money, even more if the journal is published in physical form. As such, it is logical that journals require a fee from the authors in order to make their paper open access. Moreover, most research grants will include funds for researchers to pay this fee. Despite this, most papers remain behind a paywall.

Whilst this impedes the pursuit of science, it is also to the direct detriment of the general public.In the last decade a culture of "fake news" has grown out of the easy access to the internet, where anyone can claim anything. This is not just contained to the area of current events, there are a plethora of internet sites aimed at promoting antiquated scientific theories, and distrust of scientists is growing. This is a trend that should be addressed and acted against, as it is in every country's interest to have a well-informed and educated population. Here, the question of the paywall arises spontaneously: should the latest scientific findings and results only be available to the rich or to those working in academia? How can voters trust the health or energy policy of their government if they cannot access the data or the scientific work those policies are based on? This is not just a lofty idea: people want access to research findings. In fact, scientific piracy is on the rise, and people are continuously finding ways to circumvent paywalls and gain access to what they need, but doing so places them at risk of steep fines and a criminal record. When the ultimate goal of science can be said to be to further the knowledge of the human race, having to risk arrest to access that knowledge becomes almost laughable.

In the end, the question about scientific publishing transcends economic interests and the ability to get credit for one's research. While these issues are undoubtedly important, they are not the most fundamental. At the heart of all the benefits of open and accessible research lies the question of what kind of society we would like to have, and what we want to leave behind to future generations.A world where anyone, anywhere can access the very latest research findings, review the data, methodology, and results is a more informed world. It is a world where anyone can educate themselves about issues and fields which catch their interest. It is a world where scientists are more trusted and controversial findings are more easily verified or debunked. Lastly, it is a world where science has become less of a business and more of the altruistic pursuit it was meant to be.

8   A Case for Unfettered Access

Ijeoma Priscilla Ugwuanyi

> *Access to information is a human right, but it is treated as a privilege. This has to change—and it will take all of us to make it happen.*

Erin McKiernan

Scientific knowledge is promoted by building on already existing research in any given field. Where this knowledge is not accessible, it adds to the already overwhelming challenges of creating, synthesizing and communicating scientific knowledge.

The movement to advance open access research has emerged in the last two decades as a result of two major events. The first being wide access to the internet, with the accompanied choice to have electronic academic journals rather than printed journals. This is followed by a surprisingly astronomical increase in the prices journals charge, for accessing the scientific knowledge that was neither developed by the journal owners nor edited by them [1]. This trend led to the famous "paywall" most researchers encounter while trying to access already existing research work online. The campaign for open access thus arose to enhance accessibility of research publications to scholars. A number of organizations have championed the open access movement, a list of which include but not limited to SPARC, Force11 and OpenCon.

The benefits of open access have been acknowledge by advocates since its beginning. One important benefit is the fact that, when there is open access for scholarly work, it becomes more visible to other researchers and has stronger impact on the public. Hence, authors and possible funders of open research get returns for their investment [2]. Another benefit is that open access allows institutions who cannot afford to subscribe for the expensive paywalled research, to get access to high quality research that may be hidden behind paywalls. Particular reference is made of developing countries, whose government may not be able to sponsor journal subscriptions for their universities [3].

Extrapolating from the above benefits and based on the observation of current trends, I present two major global advantages. The first is the potential of open access to advance cross-disciplinary studies. The problem of double or even multiple paywalls, also known as the serials crisis [4]—a situation where libraries cannot afford to subscribe to every scientific journal in every field—pose a severe threat to cross-disciplinary studies. Rapid and disruptive innovation in technology and digitalization has provoked conversations across many fields. For example there is a call for more conversations between business/entrepreneurship, scholars and technology/computer science scholars as more theories and assumptions in the latter field are being upended with the emergence of digital technologies [5]. The notion of who becomes an entrepreneur and where entrepreneurship can take place has changed; an entrepreneur can start his venture in his sitting room, with his or her notebook computer. More surprises are expected, given the rate at which innovation takes place. With this accelerated evolution and its consequences across disciplines, research, when open to scholars, will aid scientific responses that will benefit both theory and practice.

Secondly, the secondary effect of "closed" scientific research can be extremely disastrous. When constantly faced with a paywall, scientists may as well ignore what useful research may emerge from high-quality research that has been paywalled. A knowledge vacuum is therefore created that may result in the training of half-baked scientists and publication of incorrect research findings—the former occurring as a direct result of failure to acquire knowledge which follows inaccessible academic research, whilst the latter ensues if researchers only cite the abstract of the paywalled research in their papers as though they have read them in full. These additional challenges, with its attendant grave consequences for scientific discoveries can be averted when research is made publicly accessible.

Nevertheless, it is important to note the challenge that comes with the open access model. It could come with the danger of falling victim to predatory journals, which stand in the guise of using an open access model but seek to extort money from authors, even when the published articles have not been adequately reviewed for authors to get feedback. This occurrence could create additional ethical problems for the scientific community.

In conclusion, while the debate of which is the best model for open access research lingers, open access has come to stay, as it has great benefits for all stakeholders. It is hoped that further collaborations and conversations will resolve the differing viewpoints on the open access movement and also mitigate the negative consequences that may arise from promoting open access research.

References

1. YouTube. Piled Higher and Deeper (PHD Comics). Youtube.com., 2018. Available online: https://www.youtube.com/watch?v=9L5rVH1KGBCY (accessed on 28 February 2018).
2. Houghton, J.; Rasmussen, B.; Sheehan, P. *Economic and Social Returns on Investment in Open Archiving Publicly Funded Research Outputs*; Scholarly Publishing & Academic Resources Coalition: Washington, DC, USA, 2010.
3. Willinsky, J. *The Access Principle: The Case for Open Access to Research and Scholarship*; MIT Press: Cambridge, MA, USA, 2006.
4. Van Orsdel, L.; Born, K. Periodicals Price Survey 2005: Choosing Sides. *Libr. J.* **2005**, *130*, 43–50.
5. Nambisan, S. Digital entrepreneurship: Toward a digital technology perspective of entrepreneurship. *Entrepr. Theory Pract.* **2017**, *41*, 1029–1055. [CrossRef]

9   The Open Science Revolution

Alessandro Chiadò

Science and knowledge are day-by-day more open to everybody. No one precisely knows when this process stared, but nowadays everyone all around the word can access data and scientific results without any fee or pre-paid subscription. This phenomenon, known as "open science or open research", is due to the diffusion of social media dedicated to science, and to the development of new techniques and instruments that are able to produce huge amount of data. All of these data, that individually represent a little piece of the puzzle of knowledge, once pieced together, can potentially allow the comprehensive understanding of the mechanisms of nature as a whole, producing a real social and technological progress.

A practical example of open science is represented by the Human Genome Project, an international research effort to sequence and map the *Homo sapiens* genome. This project, completed in 2003, let us read nature's code that regulates all the aspects of the human being. Since this information is enclosed inside the genetic material of the whole population, it must be known and disseminated to the entire humanity. This is so important especially because the full understanding of this code will allow the entire scientific community to unravel physio-pathological mechanisms, and then to fight and solve diseases and health problems more efficiently, as supposed by the new prospective given by precision medicine. To reach this goal, all the information must be accessible and free to everyone, to save time and money through a global organization of the scientific research. Indeed, the huge amount of data produced by the "omics era" requires great computing capacity, whose cost can be waived only by sharing big cluster facilities and by adopting shared programs.

Open science is tightly linked to open data because they represent the same cultural shift towards more open research practice and both aspects are dependent on each other [1]. The higher the amount of available data, the higher the research shared amongst scientists, and vice versa. At the same time, if results and corresponding data are really visible to the entire community, these findings can be validated and confirmed by other groups, or, on the contrary, fake outcomes can be easily unveiled. Thanks to this mechanism open science can lead to a higher quality in the scientific research. Very often funding and careers depend only on the number of publications achieved by a researcher, instead of the real impact or quality of his work. This means that the majority of scientists try to publish their work in journals with the highest possible impact factor, despite the general condemnation of this policy that causes various detrimental effects. Due to this trend, an increasing number of rushed and messy papers were published in the last decade, even in renowned journals, resulting in a large amount of retracted papers, due to the presence of misconduct experiments, low reproducibility or even manipulated datasets and images. Without any doubt, none of these practices can lead to a real improvement of sciences and knowledge. For this reason, in 2016 the American Society for Microbiology (ASM) decided to remove the impact factor from their journals, proud of the idea that these numbers cannot assess the real significance of a research [2]. Hence, open science can be fundamental to invert this trend.

The concept of open research is then changing the way scientists collect their data, present and share their research, publish their findings, and assess the impact of their work. One of the main outcomes of this transformation is that international co-authorship is increased, because open science means also collaboration for starting new projects and for their development. At the same time, even if someone thinks that this kind of policy will be detrimental for domestic collaborations and for the economic development of single nations, the open science revolution facilitates the evolution rather than hinder it. This kind of mechanism is fundamentally evident in those research fields that have been seen as a challenge only a few years ago. For instance, now it is possible to sequence complete genomes, or to compare massive biomedical databanks, not just investigate single genes or individual cases. The unquestionable value derived by the "big data" collected by various databases spread over the globe, became then the real spring for the future of medicine, and this is plain to all. However, all of these aspects apply also to smaller and specific databases or to other fields. Certainly, environmental research is one of the other main fields that gained resources and results from the open science approach. Global warming and consequent climate change studies are the examples everyone can think about. Indeed, researchers involved in these topics were amongst the first that made use of open science and data sharing. The Intergovernmental Panel on Climate Change, or IPCC, since its establishment in 1988 gave the unique opportunity to provide rigorous and balanced scientific information related to climate change to decision-makers. The results obtained during the last thirty years would have been impossible if the environmental issues grouped under the climate change flag haven't been treated by this global community that share data and findings.

In conclusion, open science is reducing the overall costs of research activities, by making unaffordable studies and research challenges more feasible. By combining these aspects with the new methods used by researchers to share and support their results, which guarantee higher transparency but also visibility, the open science revolution is truly paving the way for the next generation of scientists and for the higher quality needed by the scientific research to solve incoming challenges.

References

1. Adams, J. *Impact of Open Science Methods and Practices on the Economics of Research and Science*; European Commission: Brussels, Belgium, 2015; ISBN 978-92-79-50444-0. [CrossRef]
2. Casadevall, A.; Bertuzzi, S.; Buchmeier, M.J.; Davis, R.J.; Drake, H.; Fang, F.C.; Gilbert, J.; Goldman, B.M.; Imperiale, M.J.; Matsumura, P.; et al. ASM journals eliminate impact factor information from journal websites. *mBio* **2016**, *7*, e01150-16. [CrossRef] [PubMed]

10   Open Research— A Supreme Way to Celebrate Your Work

Gagandeep Kaur

In today's era, research plays a significant role, not only in development, but also in introducing sound and positive changes, making the world a better place to live in. Research is of no use if it is not providing any benefits to the existing species on earth. Also, any innovation is the contribution of the researcher to that field and all other human beings should have the right to access that new idea. One mind in a particular direction can act as a drop of water, but a group of minds thinking in the same direction can emerge as a whole sea. So, why remain restricted to a droplet instead of the massive sea?

With technological and Internet advancements, the whole world has become a global village. Thanks to open research for making the development accessible to all portions of the world. Just imagine, what if Sir Thomas Edison had refused to put forth the invention of the light bulb to other people, we might have been waiting for the birth of some other Thomas Edison to come up with the invention again. What is more beautiful? To light only one home with a bulb having darkness all around or to light the whole world by distributing the bulbs and making the Earth shine brightest in the universe. Of course, to share new innovations or research at the worldwide level and to discuss its pros and cons with the fellow researchers is more beneficial. Global open research has a plethora of benefits associated with it and some of the prominent global benefits of open research are highlighted below:

1. Transparency: Open research provides a transparent view to the fellow researchers which ameliorate the chances of healthy discussions, and brings together many brains thinking in variable manners in the same research field. It nurtures the needs of the researcher as he/she grabs more by learning from other people in the same field. It also enhances the scope of worldwide recognition to high quality work by providing all the necessary credit to the authors.
2. Quality assurance: Since through open access a particular work is accessible all across the globe, automatically the particular contribution is scrutinized a number of times by other researchers and scientists. Thus, the quality of published work increases by leaps and bounds.

3.   Bridging gaps between the knowledge voids: The best way to increase knowledge is to share it. Open access provides an opportunity for the active researchers to attain more and more knowledge in a particular area by sharing with others. This is simply by working towards the development in a collaborative manner. A number of brains can work more efficiently in any field than a single brain.

4.   Shrinking the geographical distances: Gone are the days when research in a particular institution of one country remained confined to the boundaries of that institution or borders of that particular country. With the help of open access, the whole research community can benefit from the proposed work. So, distant geographical locations are just illusions in today's world. With one click of the mouse and one finger's tap on the cell-phone's screen, all the doors of knowledge are opened for you. All of this is because of the open access of research articles.

5.   Cost-effective: One of the major benefits of open access is that the extra costs incurred on the secrecy of the subject matter are reduced. It reduces the cost and fees charges for making your work accessible to more and more people. Not only this, open research is a two-sided beneficial affair in which the readers and keen aspirants also get free access to the original work.

6.   A major stone in the way of unethical activities: With suitable license policies, open access journals reduce the chances of thefts and other unethical activities. Genuine replicas of the research work are made and are circulated globally by giving proper credit to the authors.

7.   Eco-friendly: Often open access journals are accessible on the web. With the help of the electronic devices such as laptops, the use of paper has been reduced and it leads to an eco-friendly way of research.

8.   Creates a positive working environment: With research work accessible to all, a positive competitive environment is created. New approaches are not only compared to existing ones, but also the advantages of new research are highlighted in a very significant manner. It lifts the global level of knowledge and improves the standards of research.

With all the above advantages, open research acts as a glittering feather in the cap of your research, which not only provides you recognition but also reduces the chances of your work being stolen or misused. It also helps in creating good research profiles, increases the number of citations to your work. Thus, open research is far better than conducting research behind the bars of secrecy. Because ultimately, your research is of no use if it is not benefitting other people and not providing any inter- or intra-disciplinary benefits to the research community. So, open research is solely research by the researchers, for other fellow researchers and people. Although there might be some disadvantages of the open access, if it is used ethically and positively then it is a boon for the entire research community. After all, Albert Szent-Gyorgyi had rightly said, "Research is to see what everybody else has seen, and to think what nobody else has thought". So, in order to make others known to beliefs and ideas of your research, open research is best of both possible worlds.

11 The Past, Present and Future of Open Access

Syed Shan e Ali Zaidi

Open access (OA) broadly refers to free and unrestricted access to research outputs, such as journal articles and books that are available to everyone with no access fees. Over the past few years, OA has become a broad term covering essentially any research material that can benefit fellow scientists and researchers around the globe. Thus, OA may refer to anything from lab protocols, lab notes, source codes, computational tools, experimental figures and videos, to large datasets, genome sequences and even seed banks.

Availability of OA research data paves the way for immense benefits to the global community, such as (1) OA journal articles are more read and more cited than those with restricted access. (2) Open lab notes and protocols help increase the reproducibility, a nightmare in several scientific fields (psychology for example). (3) Availability of open data has provided timely disease diagnosis and has helped to accelerate solutions, for example in timely discovery of a globally spreading agricultural pathogen, blast fungus. (4) Freely available figures and videos are excellent material for lectures, making the latest knowledge readily available for students. (5) Making research data open increases the chances of getting research grants, as OA is increasingly required by funders around the world. Peer-reviewed scientific articles give researchers and scientists immediate access to the latest resources and its instant, valuable utilization. Therefore, from here onwards, I will focus only on OA journal articles.

Historically, the publishing of scientific manuscripts, especially ones with the detailed color figures, has been expensive. The general procedure of publishing worked like this: If some researchers want their article distributed broadly, they send it to one of the scientific journals. Then the journal would manage the review process, communications with reviewers, handle revisions and eventually a draft would be accepted. This draft is referred to as "peer-reviewed" draft. Then the journal would handle the typesetting, printing and the distribution of the scientific work. This procedure became an approved way of distributing reliable scientific work and science progressed very well.

But, with technological advancements, things changed. In scientific publishing, two things have really transformed, (1) digitization: now everything can be done electronically instead of printing, and (2) pricing: the publishers started increasing the price of subscriptions to many of their journals. And so, as the physical barriers were being reduced (for instance, no need to go to library to read an article), the financial barriers were growing higher. Research has shown that journal prices have increased by almost two hundred and fifty percent over the past thirty years. As an example, the fifteen most researched academic disciplines have an average price of more than a thousand dollars for one journal (for one subscription for one year). This is an average and it can be as high as forty thousand dollars for some journals [1]. These two things have supported the need for data availability, especially for people working in low income countries where not enough funds are available for libraries to buy these expensive subscriptions. The irony in OA is exemplified by a recent article that talks about the global benefits of open science in low income countries, especially in Africa. But, since it is published in a pay-walled journal, this article that advocates OA is not OA itself [2].

The current publishing system, as described above, is under massive criticism. The journals are not producing the published scientific material. They don't employ the people who write the papers; they don't even employ the people who review the papers. Scientists are paid by the government from tax-payers' money to do research and distribute that knowledge. So, if years of work by a group of government-funded scientists is compressed into a paper and that paper is not made available to the public, it is against the basic concept of scientific progress.

The future, in my opinion, is that scientists should change their practices. Publishers depend on scientists' work and not the other way around. Scientists, despite being great explorers in terms of knowledge, have been very conservative in terms of changing their practices. This has allowed journals to not respond to the community pressure towards openness. Scientists should move ahead of their double standards. They cannot support OA and want to publish their paper in restricted-access high impact factor journal at the same time. I urge all readers to read and, if they agree, to sign the San Francisco Declaration on Research Assessment (DORA: www.sfdora.org/sign/). It would be an excellent start towards breaking the monopoly and bias of the impact factor conundrum. A vast community of scientists around the world advocating OA on powerful social media platforms, such as Twitter, is a hope for change in the near future. OA preprint journals and the increasing number of research articles available on such platforms is another positive sign. I hope that the coming generation of scientists will adapt these changes and assure global availability of open research data.

Syed Shan e Ali Zaidi

References

1. Bergstrom, T.C.; Courant, P.N.; McAfee, R.P.; Williams, M.A. Evaluating Big Deal Journal Bundles. *Proc Natl Acad Sci USA* **2014**, *111*, 9425–9430. [CrossRef] [PubMed]
2. Serwadda, D.; Ndebele, P.; Grabowski, M.K.; Bajunirwe, F.; Wanyenze, R.K. Open Data Sharing and the Global South—Who Benefits? *Science* **2018**, *359*, 642–643. [CrossRef] [PubMed]

12   Open Research: Past, Present, and Future

Márió Gajdács

Open Research is essentially free, online, digital information. Open Access (OA) allows for the free and legitimate reuse of scientific results by abolishing financial and legal restrictions. OA documents can be downloaded, copied, shared, and printed with citation of the original source. The origins of the Open Access movement can be traced back to Paul Ginsparg, who installed the arXiv server at the Los Alamos National Laboratory (LAN-L), making manuscript preprints related to physics research freely available.

The enhancement of visibility and impact of scientific publications is probably the most significant benefit of Open Access publishing. Visibility refers to the likelihood with which the document can be found, relating to the extent of its reach. The results of this extended reach are the enhanced discernibility of research by other scientists and the incorporation of our results into scientific communication. This visibility of results also contributes to the global awareness related to the authors and their institutions. Open Access facilitates easier access to manuscripts over the Internet. Global availability leads to the more robust use that could increase the number of citations. Several studies confirmed that some Open Access publications may reach up to three times higher citation counts, depending on the field of research, and they will be cited much earlier. Open Access can also aid in giving precedence to authors by preprinting. While publications may be rejected by a journal, the publication of the manuscript in preprint form provides guarantees, for example, in a dispute regarding the order of materials published or a patent.

Digital documents are available directly and at any time, they are easily stored, copied, forwarded and printed, thus, they can be the basis of new scientific achievements. They are not subject to restrictions of length (unlike for articles published under the classical publishing platform), with the additional opportunity to refer to other materials (e.g., audio and video content, supplementary documents, raw data files, software) that serve the documentation, illustration, and credibility of the results. The publication speed of digital documents is also significantly faster, since in Open Access publications, managing editors usually set a short deadline for publishing an accepted manuscript. Digital documents facilitate joint work and enable web-based collaboration in producing research reports.

Open Access supports the supply of information from a technical perspective—since the opportunity for direct access means that data procurement and related time loss is not an issue anymore—on the other hand, with the increasing number of openly accessible documents, the acquisition of information is simpler, faster and more authentic. Long-term archiving of documents on servers is guaranteed, which is not always the case when sharing research data on personal or institutional websites. The permanent availability of texts is assured by identifiers (such as the Digital Object Identifier system), whose accuracy is independent of the actual storage location of the document.

Since the 'Serials Crisis', there are fewer journals available in university libraries due to the high subscription costs. As a result, libraries are forced to cancel their long-standing subscriptions. For example, the costs of some journals in medicine, science and technology have quadrupled over the past twelve years, while the budget of libraries has remained practically unchanged. Open Access publishing may offer a solution to the resulting lack of information. The results of publicly funded research are freely available to the public to access, and there is no need for the scientific institutions (e.g., universities, National Academies of Sciences) to buy or repurchase them from the journal publishers. Criticism is often heard that the public must fund research three times: scholars paid from public funds perform research and publish, their results are evaluated by scholars in the peer review process, who are also get paid by the public sector, and institutions need to buy from publishers to close this scientific 'communication circle'.

Interconnecting scientific information sources fosters the internationalization of science, and Open Access has a key role in this process. The globally free access to OA content enables less fortunate countries to access relevant and up-to-date scientific information for research purposes, but also for their everyday lives. The Open Access movement helps to overcome the 'digital divide' and contributes to all countries having access to research results in the world's scientific community. Texts written in the national languages continue to play a leading role in the field of humanities and social sciences. However, if a foreign language text is available online for free, there is a growing chance that someone will notice it, even if it doesn't have an abstract in English. The simultaneous international presence of scientific documents leads to an increased chance of collaboration between scientists and accelerates the process of research itself, as authors can receive instant feedback from their respective peers. Open Access also promotes interdisciplinary cooperation, since it allows for scientist to notice current information coming from other areas that they may not encountered in articles published under the classical publishing platform. In an increasingly complex world, with multi-layered questions in science or otherwise, Open Access publishing gives the ideal framework for joint solutions to hard-to-answer research questions and problems.

13   Taking the Leap: The Benefits of Open Science

Simon Morand-Beaulieu

We, as scientists, are problem solvers. When we find something that does not work, we think about a way to fix it. This might seem like a very straightforward way to describe ours jobs as scientists, but problem solving is common to all scientists, no matter the field. However, when the problem is about science itself, how do we fix it? Let's face it, most research teams work *in silo*, not sharing their hard-acquired data. Scientists perform *pro bono* reviews of scientific papers for billionaire publishing corporations. And authors of those reviewed papers will probably never know who did that peer review. Even more sadly, scientists will publish their work in scientific publications which they sometimes cannot even access. Open science has the possibility to fix a lot of what is wrong in science. This could be achieved in three different ways, which could have major benefits to the academic community: open data, open review, and open access.

In a few decades, open data should have become the norm rather than the exception. This principle has so much to offer. Of course, some data cannot be shared, such as private information or sensitive data. But sharing adnominalized data offers the opportunity of worldwide collaborations and would maximize transdisciplinarity. Meta-analytical research is an area that would greatly benefit from globalized open data. Individual participant data meta-analyses have many advantages over traditional meta-analyses [1], but are difficult to conduct given the limited access to individual participant data from other studies. Having access to such data would allow scientists to make much more advanced analyses and expand the impact of their findings. Furthermore, it is an open secret that research funding is critical in many areas. Since an important proportion of research funding is used toward data acquisition, open data would allow to maximize the usage of acquired data, and therefore make an optimal use of taxpayers' money. It would also allow scientists with limited funding to pursue research on publicly shared data.

Open review should also become more frequent in the coming years. Scientists should not hide behind anonymity to criticize the work of another scientist. In my mind, open reviews would lead to more honest and constructive comments. The review system used by Frontiers journals constitutes a step in the right direction. By having a platform where authors can exchange with the reviewers, it is easier to understand what is wanted by the reviewers and how to perform the required changes. Authors can explain why they made a certain choice and could therefore modify a reviewer's recommendation. Such back-and-forth communication between authors and reviewers can lead to a significantly improved paper. Review reports should also be published alongside papers. By knowing that their names and review would be published, reviewers would be highly rigorous during the peer review process. It would also allow the reader to understand the creative process that led to the final version of the article, as they would find useful information in the review report [2].

Finally, an important way toward globalized open science is the open access to scientific publication. Open access to science should be mandatory. Most research is financed by taxpayers, through federal funding agencies. It is a nonsense that those who pay for research don't have access to it [3]. I feel that most scientists agree that the open access system constitute the best avenue for the future of science and should therefore be prioritized. Yet, for various reasons, scientists' old habits are difficult to change. If we could close all existing journals and start on new foundations, I think that scientists would choose the open access system over the traditional publishing system. From my point of view, it appears that two factors may actually limit the willingness of scientists to publish in open access journals: impact factors that can be lower than in other journals and publishing costs. Even though the usefulness of the impact factor is largely debated, it remains used by many scientists to choose the journal where they wish to submit a manuscript. For open access journals to gain ground on traditional journal, much must be done regarding the prestige and impact of publications. This could be performed by using new metrics to measure publications' performance and journal impact, instead of the highly criticized journal impact factor. But this is a whole other debate.

Paying for publication is a mandatory feature of open-access publishing. Scientists understand why they must pay, and they agree with the principle. But in practice, when comes the time to submit a manuscript, saving some money might become tempting, given the precarity that many scientists must deal with. A solution to this problem could be provided by universities. By providing a monetary incentive or a compensation, they would encourage scientists to publish more in open access journals. By progressively cancelling subscriptions to major publishing companies, they could offer such incentives. For example, through a recent agreement between Frontiers, the University of Vienna and the Austrian Science Fund, article processing charges are now covered for Austrian scientists who wish to publish their findings in Frontiers open access journals. This type of policy, which constitutes a major step toward open science, should be emulated by other countries.

All in all, open data, open review, and open access can all have a positive impact on scientific research. It depends on us, as scientists, to take the necessary measures to implement these principles in our research and publishing habits. After all, we might be the ones who would benefit the most from it.

References

1. Riley, R.D.; Lambert, P.C.; Abo-Zaid, G. Meta-analysis of individual participant data: rationale, conduct, and reporting. *BMJ* **2010**, *340*, c221. [CrossRef] [PubMed]
2. Ross-Hellauer, T.; Deppe, A.; Schmidt, B. Survey on open peer review: Attitudes and experience amongst editors, authors and reviewers. *PLoS ONE* **2017**, *12*, e0189311. [CrossRef] [PubMed]
3. Malakoff, D. Opening the Books on Open Access. *Science* **2003**, *302*, 550–554. [CrossRef] [PubMed]

14   A Free Piece of Cake

Gianluca Cidonio

Being a final year PhD student in the UK is not easy. Challenges in modern research seem to be insuperable not only in the UK but in most of the Western world. My institute gave me access to countless journals and articles paying quite a considerable amount of fees to let me have this privilege. Yet, this is not enough. I always need that one article which is not there. I have to place an interlibrary loan, or an online article request on the system. The article usually arrives after one week, too late for all my literature research. Sometimes even later than that, I receive the temporary access to a PDF version for just few hours and cannot fully explore its content. I found this process quite frustrating, but this is not because my institute library is not efficient—librarians are helpful and accommodating—but it is often impossible to read a single line of a desired article without paying a large fee and have trouble to ask for a temporary access to this.

I must admit being guilty of using the help from colleagues in other universities to quickly obtain a research paper that is essential for me to read through immediately. I have most certainly found benefit from articles that were shared on platforms such as bioRxiv (pre-print platform for biologists) and Researchgate (social network for scientists). The latter is gaining momentum among scientists all over the world that can share and communicate their latest results, asking for suggestions and protocols useful with their research. Social media for researchers are becoming essential in my studies. Community platforms where I can search and download published articles uploaded by the publishing researchers is starting to be crucial in my everyday "latest article" search routine. Twitter is recently becoming much appreciated. Scientists can post their articles on social networks like this (certainly worth mentioning LinkedIn and sometimes Facebook) and tweet about their findings, increasing visibility and knowledge that is often translated in consequent citations. For this, Twitter is a fantastic tool for researchers. I am looking at Twitter every day to increase my knowledge of the latest article published in my field and tweeting about my research. Social media are useful because every day more senior researchers are signing up and sharing their latest interests in papers and funding available. Looking at this, I am personally inspired and tend to look at what they publish and investigate these funding opportunities that might be of my interest. Twitter's wide-open door on research communities is a tremendous chance for global researchers to interact and connect building up a real source of information for science and research.

These thoughts drive me back to a couple of years ago when I have been visiting a German research institute for some time of collaborative work with a group of similar research interests. There, I have experienced a new freedom: They were subscribed to journals which I did not have access to back in the UK. At the same time, German researchers were experiencing my identical issue, as they could not access journals that I could read in the UK instead. During that time a true shared knowledge was possible only thanks to the fact that I was there. This was liberating. I could research articles which I was looking for for months and never got to read, explore journals that published interesting research for my area of interest. This was simply amazing. Indeed, we manage to outsource and share reciprocal benefits of the use of different research journal platforms. From this, a new idea came out and we started working on something new, never seen before, a new biomaterial of orthopaedic use that could be mixed with stem cells, printed in three dimensions and then implanted into patients affected by moderate or severe bone loss. We managed to further investigate this new material and get out with a simple, yet efficient and innovative technique.

I believe that my personal experience that I listed here is the perfect summary of what "open research" means, as something available to everyone to benefit from and that can further advance the scientific knowledge.

Open access research is not a recent achievement, but lately it has become an essential aim for many journals. As an urgent need, numerous scientists are starting to publish papers via this open system. Being open and free has drastically increased articles visibility. Particularly on Twitter, researchers are posting free of prejudice their latest open access papers for people to download and further retweet and share. This is particularly useful not only for scientists who crave for the latest news on their research field but also for lay people who dare to sneak-peek the scientific innovations before being released by the press. An open article is more than just a scientific report but can be a free "piece of cake" for everyone to enjoy, a research work that is available and freely shared with other peers looking forward to doing research for the mere reason of further advancing world knowledge. Research groups are always more often close with secret protocols that cannot be replicated. However, research that cannot be repeated somewhere else using same resources and protocols is not true research. What is the purpose of this if someone on the other side of the globe cannot use the protocol listed (or partially listed) on your research paper to reproduce what you have created or discovered and maybe save a life? Openness should bring people to collaborate and share, to get more interested in each other's work, free of boundaries of outsourcing new possibilities and unexplored approaches to science. This should bring collaborations, a free exchange of ideas and ways of investigating science that can only be beneficial for the whole scientific community. Only with clear and transparent research methods that can, as a result, show open outcomes, we can further improve our understanding of the reality and gain boundless benefit for humankind.

15   A Spec of Research to Which Anyone Can Add

Rebecca von Hellfeld

The Philosophical Transactions of the Royal Society first appeared 1665 and is the oldest journal still in print, ringing in a new journalistic era focussed on the scientific integrity of each individual paper, rather than combining efforts to drive scientific discoveries faster. While this may have ensured the development of the today's strong scientific foundation, many have begun to consider it outdated. Just as most longstanding traditions, it is time to reconsider its value to society and, where necessary, make alterations. One criticism is that the results obtained by research are not freely accessible and most data is kept secret, slowing the speed of discovery considerably. A step towards easier access and more collaboration was recently taken when the Gates Foundation—donating $ 4bn to scientific research each year—imposed that all results and papers generated in projects they funded must be made freely available to the public [1,2]. Other foundations have made similar requests, thus making them a driving force into an open research future. This concept, also called "open research", or "open science", has been talked about since the 1990s, but progress towards it had been slow. The central aim is to make the research methodology, along with the data and results, freely accessible, allowing a more collaborative approach to research [3]. Whilst there are various different takes on how to apply this to today's scientific community, it seems prudent to understand what we stand to gain from this approach first.

Most non-commercial research these days is funded by the government, meaning the tax-payers' money is invested into scientific work. One can thus argue that since we fund the research, we should have free access to its results, but sadly, increasingly high subscription fees are standing in the way for most [1]. One can also argue that with the time spent on the publishing process (tailoring a paper to the journal's needs, peer-reviewing, editing, re-editing, and finally publishing it), a lot of findings never reach the light of day. This means that the money would be utilised more effectively if there was not such a high hurdle looming at the end [4]. However, one should keep in mind the real possibility of misunderstanding or misusing scientific results. Many lack the proper scientific training to correctly interpret the results, leading to misconceptions or (unwarranted) fear [5]. When considering misuse of scientific results, a prominent example is the creation of a H5N1 influenza (better known as the "bird flu") strain by Dutch researchers, altering its structure and making it easily transmitted between ferrets [5,6]. Humans may not seem to share many similarities with ferrets, but any previous influenza strain that was infectious among ferrets had a similar impact on human health [7]. Making results like these publicly available increases the risk of misuse [8]. Most people lack the correct training to interpret the results and outcomes of research correctly, leading to issues such as unwarranted panic [5].

From a researcher's perspective there are clear benefits to be gained from open science. One, which will sound like music to the ears of all scientists who have battled the process of publishing a paper in the past, is how much faster papers could be published [3]. Rather than wasting months looking for a suitable journal, formatting the paper to their liking, being reviewed, and then having to edit and re-edit, open access would be a fast-track way to publishing. Now the work would be selected based on its objectives, data and provided information, not whether its style suits the journal. Peer-reviewers would then be invited via the platform, with openly stated conflicts of interest, allowing the focus to fall back on the primary goal: helping authors improve their work with constructive feedback [8]. Currently, reviewing papers is viewed as a tedious task with little incentive, thus being neglected by many. With open science, however, reviews would receive their own identifier, thus making them citable and allowing the referee to benefit from the process as much as the paper's author(s) [9]. This would also silence the concern regarding anonymous peer-reviewers purposefully stalling to gain a head's start, or, conversely, being especially lenient in some cases, creating an equivalent retaliation atmosphere, rather than an unbiased assessment of the paper [10]. However, researchers view open research sceptically, since many a reputation was built on journals such as *Nature* to select and review the papers they published, making it a "stamp of approval" of sorts, to be published in it [8]. Since open research entails that everything can be submitted for publication, this prestigious position would no longer be given, and all papers views as equal. Another argument against open science may be that open source leads to unsorted information, which in turn overwhelms the scientists looking for specific data. However, these worries may easily be soothed when looking at the current direction of open science, since it is in a constant state of change and improvement [11]. Lastly, the fact that more people have access to the publication also allows for increased citation and usage, thus allowing scientific advancements to accelerate.

It has become obvious that we are in a transitionary state between the well-known, rigid, journal publishing and the flexible open science approach, and that we must embrace this change if we want to gain anything from it [10].

Whilst there are many good points to be made for the old system, one must keep in mind that technology and interconnectedness are key factors nowadays, and these should not be kept out of the scientific community when it comes to collaborating and publishing [12]. A prime example for the necessity of open science is the synthesis of a cheaper, more potent treatment for schistosomiasis (a rather unpleasant illness caused by flatworms and currently affecting more than 200 million people) [4]. This has driven down the research and development cost, which has often been the breaking point of many projects [13]. Here, the focus was no longer on the race against other research teams to develop the drug, but rather the communal race against the disease.

References

1. The Economist. *The Findings of Medical Research Are Disseminated Too Slowly*; The Economist Group Limited: London, UK, 2017; Available online: https://www.economist.com/news/science-and-technology/21719438-about-change-findings-medical-research-are-disseminated-too (accessed on 10 October 2018).
2. The Wellcome Trust Foundation. Open Research. Available online: https://wellcome.ac.uk/what-we-do/our-work/open-research (accessed on 10 October 2018).
3. Vitae, Realising the Potential of Researchers. What Is Open Research? Available online: https://www.vitae.ac.uk/doing-research/open-research-and-open-researchers/what-is-open-research (accessed on 10 October 2018).
4. Butler, D. Open-Source Science Takes on Neglected Disease. Nature News, 2010. Available online: http://www.nature.com/news/2010/100204/full/news.2010.50.html (accessed on 10 October 2018).
5. Enserink, M. Scientists Brace for Media Storm around Controversial Flu Studies, 2011. Science Magazine. Available online: https://www.sciencemag.org/news/2011/11/scientists-brace-media-storm-around-controversial-flu-studies (accessed on 10 October 2018).
6. Malakoff, D., Sr. U.S. Lawmaker Leaps into H5N1 Flu Controversy, 2012. Science Magazine. Available online: http://www.sciencemag.org/news/2012/03/senior-us-lawmaker-leaps-h5n1-flu-controversy (accessed on 10 October 2018).
7. Cohen, J.; Enserink, M.; Malakoff, D. A Central Researcher in the H5N1 Flu Debate Breaks His Silence, 2012. Science Magazine. Available online: https://www.sciencemag.org/news/2012/01/central-researcher-h5n1-flu-debate-breaks-his-silence (accessed on 10 October 2018).
8. Davis, P.M.; Walters, W.H. The impact of free access to the scientific literature: A review of recent research. *J. Med. Libr. Assoc.* **2011**, *99*, 208–217. [CrossRef] [PubMed]

9. Woelfle, M.; Olliaro, P.; Todd, M.H. Open science is a research accelerator. *Nat. Chem.* **2011**, *3*, 745–748. Available online: https://www.nature.com/articles/nchem.1149 (accessed on 10 October 2018). [CrossRef] [PubMed]

10. Joint, N. The Antaeus column: Does the "open access" advantage exist? A librarian's perspective. *Libr. Rev.* **2008**, *58*, 477–481. [CrossRef]

11. Björk, B.-C.; Solomon, D. Open access versus subscription journals: A comparison of scientific impact. *BMC Med.* **2012**, *10*, 73. [CrossRef] [PubMed]

12. Dorta-González, P.; Santana-Jiménez, Y. Prevalence and citation advantage of gold open access in the subject area of the Scopus database. *Res. Eval.* **2018**, *27*, 1–15. [CrossRef]

13. Maurer, S.M.; Rai, A.; Sali, A. Finding cures for tropical diseases: Is open source an answer? *PLoS Med.* **2004**, *1*, 56. Available online: https://www.ncbi.nlm.nih.gov/pmc/articles/PMC539047/ (accessed on 10 October 2018). [CrossRef] [PubMed]

16 The 3 Cs of Open Research: Canalization, Communication and Collaboration

José Jaramillo Ortiz

If we look retrospectively, the current trends in the field of science are now making an enormous effort in constructing a more open research network in comparison with the seventies or eighties, where only the elites could access prestigious journals. The big deal in order to break this barrier has been, in the last three decades, the way in which the science—and its production—could be more tangible to the end-user.If any human activity were engaged in breaking down barriers, it would be science. But the goals seem to be harder when the obstacles are within. The idea of effective open research, capable of including all the actors, is a matter that involves the complete scientific community in a permanent debate about how to manage some weak points. Here we examine them.

1. Canalization of the Information. Pay-Per-View vs. Paper View

Basically, an open access journal provides online information which is free of charge for the public. If this 'online information' concerns scientific results and 'public' means the investigators, generally an academic institution pays an additional fee. It may sound unbelievable, but many scientists do not know that their institutions negotiate these licenses. At a glance, open access has been led the governments—not only to see where the results of their funds are, but also whether these outcomes are available to the educational institutions sustained by the same governments. In addition, open access contributes to accelerating investigations, making visible the findings which might be situated in the confines of the globe. Does this circle close harmoniously? Apart from the good, open access has its bad. While many open access journals are careful and rigorous in their publication processes, some others are of dubious origin—with predatory intentions, including academic journals. They try to persuade readers and researchers to publish, offering them the advantage of open access. As a result, papers get published without a critical look. This situation is harmful for the advancement of science.

2. Communication of the Information. English Language: The Language of Science

If we were in the late 18th century and dressed according to that time, on board an iconic transatlantic ship, we would have communicated in French. However, in the 21st century, it is a fact that French has definitely lost the language culture battle. Nowadays, more people speak English as a second language than native English-speakers who speak it as a first language. Is this good news? At least for science it is. Then, the composition of this place transports me to a room, where Asians, Africans, Caucasians and Hispanics amongst others understand the same concepts and exchange opinions with the speaker who gives us his dissertation in English. At the end of the day, the relaxed social meeting in the mezzanine level of the hotel happens without any cultural impediment: the verbal communication has been perfectly naturalized. It is so taken for granted that English is the language of science that we do not reflect even for a while on the powerful meaning of communication.

3. Collaboration through Information: The Bridge of Sighs in the Scientific World

Finally, the importance of communication strengthens peer collaborations. Nevertheless, this is not taken for granted everywhere. There are considerable serious limitations for scientific progress in middle-income countries. Only those underdeveloped countries that assume the transparency of including clear and targeted scientific programs in their policies will be considered as a part of extensive consortia networks. An example of this is Horizon 2020 which, apart from facilitating open access research, extends the opportunities beyond the frontiers of the 'old continent'. This means a blunt case of openness to knowledge and innovation. Science is a social phenomenon; it is not an individual construction. Communications and collaborations are both social phenomena in this human activity as well. If we do not have a common understanding of what is necessary in order to tear down the walls that encloses open research, then the global benefits will be only circumscribed to those countries and companies that guard the knowledge as if they were the 'Knights Templar'. Consequently, the potential benefits will not be global.

In conclusion, I do believe that what is mentioned here as the 3 Cs are the global benefits of open research. Canalization of the communication. Communication for collaboration. As the legend of the Knight Templar tells, we also have a 'treasure' to protect, contributing to an inclusive, effective and open research.

17   Open Research: A Gateway to Scientific Outreach and Innovation

Abel Abera Negash

For someone from Africa who is trying his best to participate in the modern realms of research, there is nothing like the feeling of being restricted from access to literature. In most cases of restricted access, what is available will only be the abstract, and the researcher would either have to think of citing the article by picking few points available in the abstract or move on and search for articles will full access. The former will create misrepresentation of research data and the latter will mean more chance for articles with full access to be cited.

There are also occasions where new information based on a scientific publication will appear in an online platform, which could be a magazine or some other website in which a link will be provided to the original article. Yet again, restricted access means that someone with a curiosity will be held back because he cannot access the scientific work. He would inadvertently be obliged then to solely depend on the views of the reporter.

For someone who has gone through both of the aforementioned experiences, open access will mean freedom and fulfillment. It will certainly create opportunities for more shared knowledge and skills. It will also give him/her the opportunity to look into the perspectives of people from another side of the world, learn from the methodologies they used and look for ways of applying them in his/her local context.

What about the researcher that publishes on an open access platform? Doesn't it mean more visibility for his work? Indeed, yes [1]. Since citation breeds citation, it means increased access and dissemination of his/her work, increased recognition in the wider scientific world, and perhaps a door for opening additional career opportunities. This will not be limited to people involved in research, but it also means open access to the public and more chances of public engagement.

Open access also means more transparency. In a time where more and more articles are now being retracted because of plagiarism, data fabrication, redundancy and ethical issues [2–4], open access will more or less help to ensure adherence to ethical principles and to monitor transparency.

What we often also forget is that most research funding comes from taxpayers' money [5] and restricting access means in some ways restricting the right of another researcher and the public to access something that has been produced with their own money. It is also through openness, public engagement and knowledge sharing that we can, in the end, affect policy changes and implementation of scientific outputs.

Globally, open access therefore means increased knowledge sharing, networking, collaboration, innovation, prosperity and a better future for the world.

References

1. Research Information Network (RIN). Nature Communications: Citation analysis. **2014**, 2, 1–6.
2. Singh, H.P.; Mahendra, A.; Yadav, B.; Singh, H.; Arora, N.; Arora, M. A Comprehensive Analysis of Articles Retracted between 2004 and 2013 from Biomedical Literature—A Call for Reforms. *J. Tradit. Complement. Med.* **2014**, *4*, 136–139. [CrossRef] [PubMed]
3. Hesselmann, F.; Graf, V.; Schmidt, M.; Reinhart, M. The visibility of scientific misconduct: A review of the literature on retracted journal articles. *Curr. Sociol.* **2017**, *65*, 814–845. [CrossRef] [PubMed]
4. Steen, R.G.; Casadevall, A.; Fang, F.C. Why Has the Number of Scientific Retractions Increased? *PLoS ONE* **2013**, *8*, e68397. [CrossRef]
5. Correa, P. *Public Expenditure Reviews in Science, Technology, and Innovation*; World Bank Group: Washington, DC, USA, 2014.

18   Open Access and Traditional Journal Publications Assessment

Pedram Asef

While open access (OA) research avoids any type of restriction such as paywalls and political matters, it is still problematic for numerous students and scientists to reach scientific resources in many developing countries. Global access to OA publications spreads knowledge which provides a platform that can be built upon. The positive influence of OA availability presents a significant acceleration to scientific enquiry worldwide. This article introduces the advantages for each affected group including: students, residents of developing countries, engineering and medical researchers, authors and publishers, as well as entrepreneurs. Additionally, the impact of OA research on higher visibility and citation in various fields of science is discussed.

In the past, lack of authenticity and little accessibility internet resulted in large expenses related to time-consuming publication and distribution. The popularization of electronic publishing has created many benefits related to increased internet availability and improved search ability based on Berlin and Bethesda declarations [1] throughout the world. Information restrictions in any form have predominantly affected particular groups of people such as: students, residents of developing countries, researchers, authors, publishers, and entrepreneurs. Although students experience the largest individual impact related to their need to access research sources despite institutional divestment in increasingly over-priced journals, residents of developing countries experience a broader impact over the entire population. Affected people in developing countries include everything from students, researchers, and doctors, to the general public who self-educate using the internet as a didactic tool. Intuitions in developing countries can only afford access to a small fraction of research journals due to the restricted budget they have been granted. The research process and publication both have their own life cycles, terminated by an end goal of peer review and publication. This process is mainly based on writing a proposal, followed by planning and executing a study, and subsequent analysis, data management, and publication. However, research articles also rely on idea conception, and a thorough process of generation, communication, evaluation, verification, implementation, influence, and finally a potential to inspire future investigation and innovation. Today, it is inevitable that the open access (OA) movement results in a higher rate of readership, global presence, increased accessibility and wider collaborations. This relies in part on both citations that highlight related work and better public engagement to present new research topics. None of this is possible without quick feedback, to which continued reflection and heightened interdisciplinary conversation are vital [1–3]. Figure 1 illustrates a simplified flowchart regarding how the research process and OA publications share a joint information cycle. It should be mentioned that OA publications are generally classified into two types: gold and green. A number of additional types such as hybrid, delayed, short-time, selected, and partial have been defined. Considerable primary advantages of OA in comparison with traditional publications are demonstrated to be only due to access restriction exemptions in Figure 1. OA scholarly publishing has been distinguished by type (green, gold, etc.) related to the intended viewing platform. OA contents offer free accessibility to general and specialized audiences which enrich readership and results in a wider audience.

Increased global visibility in both developed and developing countries leads to a higher rate of citation and metrics and a greater likelihood of international research efforts. Researchers study others' research and work to become informed on two relevant skillful scientific outcomes and movements relevant to their field which can result in international collaborations in both institutional and individual disciplines.

Author and publisher satisfaction play a significant role to determining a successful progress from ideation to publication. Figure 2 presents authors' satisfaction metrics in relation to the OA work procedure. Most OA journals provide a quick revision of submitted manuscripts with a rigorous and transparent peer-review process which results in a less time and resource dependent publication. Additionally, article-level metrics of each individual paper in a summary format are available on the webpage of OA journals. This includes details such as views, citations, downloads, discussions, and recommendations.

The European development of the OA market through 2020 is an outstanding model to deliver widespread OA throughout the continent, in which a growth rate of 25% is required [3]. The path has distinguished several valuable policy interventions to reach this goal in Europe; however, the identified scenario is applicable to the global OA system as given:

- Offsetting of subscription and OA charges,
- Fortifying consortia and gathering collective action,
- Enhancement of repository underlying foundation,
- Advancement of changes in author behavior and motivations,

- Endorsing Gold frameworks without article publishing costs (APCs) and upgrading clearness of publication expenses,
- Elaborating mechanisms to monitor OA content.

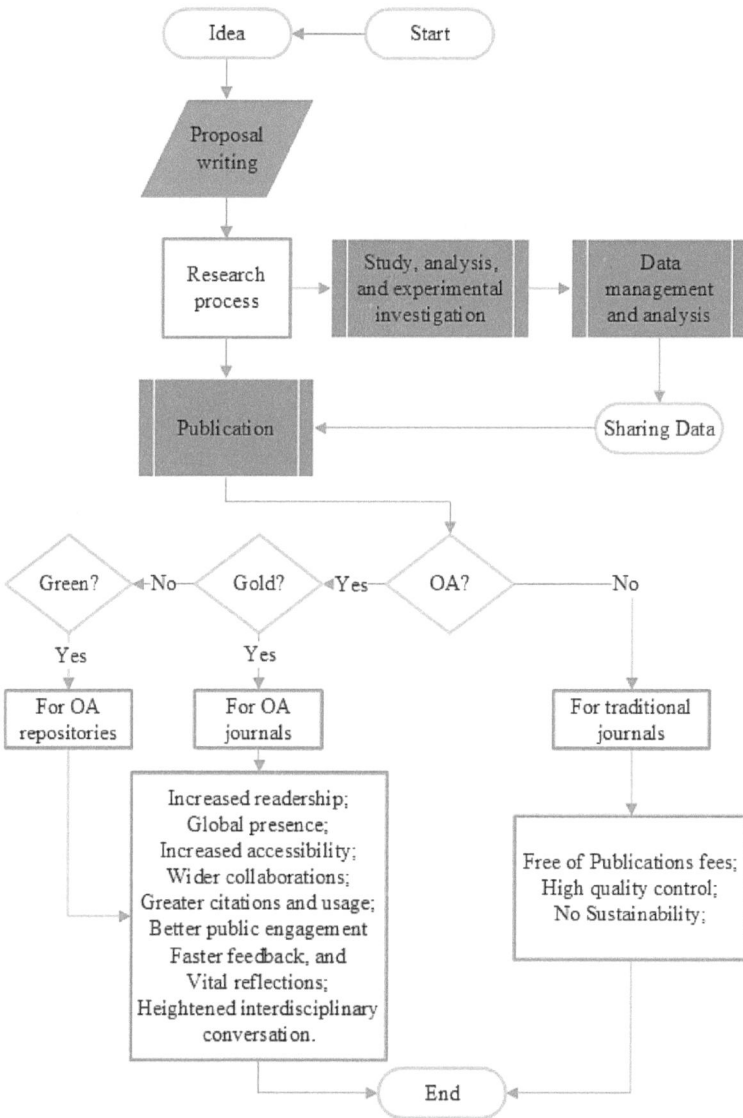

Figure 1. Simplified research and publication flowchart.

Figure 2. Authors and reader satisfaction metrics.

The future underlying barriers of OA journals market development based on the mentioned European model findings can be accomplished through the following suggested considerations such as:

- Increasing the proportion of research which relies on quick decision and publication with appropriate quality controls,
- Enhancing a competitive as well as sustainable OA market worldwide,
- Decreasing APCs (especially Gold pathway) in the favor of authors through hardcopy revenue and subscribing individuals or institutions.

References

1. Kanjilal, U.; Kumar Das, A. *Introduction to Open Access*; United Nations Educational, Scientific and Cultural Organization (UNESCO): Paris, France, 2015; pp. 1–81. ISBN 978-92-3-100074-4.
2. Mishra, S.; Kumar Das, A. *Sharing Your Work in Open Access*; United Nations Educational, Scientific and Cultural Organization (UNESCO): Paris, France, 2015; pp. 1–35. ISBN 978-92-3-100083-6.
3. Johnson, R.; Fosci, M.; Chiarelli, A.; Pinfield, S.; Jubb, M. *Towards a Competitive and Sustainable OA Market in Europe—A Study of the Open Access Market and Policy Environment*; Research Consulting: Nottingham, UK, 2017; pp. 1–76.

19   Science Should Not Be Kept Behind Paywalls

Stefan Stošić

Access to knowledge is basic human right, according to the United Nations Declaration of Human Rights. But we should ask ourselves: Does everyone have equal access to knowledge? No, they do not. The majority of today's world knowledge is archived in many science journals. Those journals form Alexandria's library of our time. And most of the shelves in that library are locked. They are behind a paywall. If you would like to read/download/print some of their articles, you (or your institution/government) have to pay. Subscription fees are high (both for individuals and institutions) so not everyone has the possibility to read about the newest scientific discoveries. There are assumptions that the profit of scientific publishers goes up to 40%. That's more than the profit of the oil industry, which is considered highly profitable.

Science has passed through radical transformation in the last several centuries, from an activity of curious, sometimes bored, wealthy individuals to the system that engages many stakeholders: scientists, research institutions, governments, publishers, etc.

Until recently, the dominant model of publishing scientific results was:

1. countries fund the research with public money (collected through taxes);
2. scientists do the research and write their results in the form of a journal article;
3. scientists submit their article (for free) to a journal;
4. scientific publishers accept and publish articles in journals but demand transfer of researcher's copyright to the publishers;
5. as a consequence of copyright transfer, publishers demand from us to pay subscription fee (individual or institutional) in order to access those journal articles.

In this process, countries pays twice—when they finance the research and again for accessing journal articles. Who benefits the most in this business model? The publishers. This explains the 40% profit margin. And that's not the end of the story—in past 30 years subscription fees have risen by 250% [1]! That represents an unsustainable and greedy business model, in which even rich universities (e.g., Harvard, the richest of them all) are unable to pay for access to the scientific literature.

As a response to this business model of scientific publishing, twenty years ago an open access movement was born. Open access "refers to online research outputs that are free of all restrictions on access and free of many restrictions on use (e.g., copyright and license restrictions)" [2]. In simpler words, open access means that people (scientists or laymen) from all around the world can freely read, print, send, download and use scientific articles for analysis and creation of new knowledge. In the very core of this movement is scientific and cultural progress of human civilization. Open access is tightly connected with open research, which is equal to open science. Open science "is consisted of six commonly accepted pillars: open data, open access, open methodology, open source, open peer review and open education" [3].

Benefits of Open Research

Better and Transparent Science

Open research will allow that many of the proposed hypotheses and published discoveries can be tested and verified/opposed. The reproducibility potential will be increased. Science makes sense only when its theories are submitted to various tests. In that way, the best theories can stand out as valid and correct and misleading ones can be discarded. With open data any interested party can reassess previous findings and conclusions or find some other valid conclusion. There will be fewer scientific hoaxes when data are open and can be analyzed by other colleagues.

Wider Impact and Citation of Published Results

Results published in open access journals are available to all. All you need is a computer connected to the Internet and nowadays the Internet is present in almost all parts of the world. The results will be available to the professionals outside academia (schools, hospitals, etc.) but also to small businesses and Non-Government Organizations (NGOs). It can result in new innovations and can boost entrepreneurship.

Decreasing the Difference in Science Between Developed and Developing Countries

The world is still fighting with poverty and if we want to help low and middle income countries to escape from the claws of poverty and misery, we should endorse open science. In a time where we have this divide into the Global North and the Global South, it is unacceptable and unimaginable to keep science closed. Right now there is a big gap between developed and developing countries in any aspect, including science. Open research can help to bridge that gap, through open articles but also through potential collaborations that can be established once the existing paywalls are down. From that collaboration both poles, South and North, can benefit.

Predatory publishers and practices will become less problematic than they are now, because scientists will choose well-known and established open access publishers. Libraries and governments could allocate some amount of money they give for journal subscriptions to some other activities.

In these times where global inequalities are on the rise, it is certainly not fair that governments invest public money into scientific research which will be published in journals where scientists have to pay again to access them. In that way, the inequality gap becomes wider and deeper and in the end just a few dozen people have benefits from the work of millions of researchers. Science is (in most cases) financed with public funds and its results should be available to the public. Science behind paywalls is in the interest of journal/publisher owners. We don't need another case of an unfortunate Aaron Swartz to prove that.

It is important to adopt a new business model that redefines the current state of scientific publishing. That model should take care of interests of all stakeholders. Science is based on previous discoveries. You have to "stand on the shoulders of giants" (Sir Isaac Newton) in order to see further. Those giants are scientists and their research. And in order to see scientific research, they should be free and open. It's that simple. Open science strives towards and is a path towards a more equal society. And we cannot have an equal society if we have any walls, including paywalls.

References

1. Electronic Froniter Foundation (EEF). Open Access. EFF. Available online: https://www. eff.org/issues/open-access (accessed on 10 October 2018).
2. Suber, P. Open Access Overview. Available online: Earlham.edu (accessed on 28 February 2018).
3. Watson, M. When will 'open science' become simply 'science'? *Genome Biol.* **2015**, *16*, 101. [CrossRef] [PubMed]

20   Open Research: A Transformative Way Towards Collaboration, Sharing and Dissemination of Knowledge

Lipi Chhaya

In the long history of humankind (and animal kind too) those who learned to collaborate and improvise most effectively have prevailed.

Charles Darwin

The true purpose of an education is to enhance the self-worth, dignity, and satisfaction of an individual through attainment and dissemination of knowledge. The Internet is the most ingenious and innovative technology of the present era. It has paved the way for knowledge sharing through open research. An open research can be defined as a research work which is ubiquitously accessible to everyone. The work published under open access policy can be re-used with proper citation as well as accreditation of accessed literature. Open research exterminates various barriers such as subscriptions, price per article, licensing fees, and permissions. There are numerous benefits of open research as depicted below.

1. Improved Citation of Research Work

The statistical findings depicted in the report published on Nature Communications [1] illustrate that open access documents are referred and cited thrice more than access controlled research papers. Thus, open research expands the reach as well as recognition of work. Enhanced citations and recognition given to distinctive research endeavors are decisive for the establishment of authors as experts in their respective fields.

2. Enhancement of Interdisciplinary Sharing and Research Endeavors

The evolution of technology has crossed the barrier of an explicit field. Open research is the significant factor behind interdisciplinary research endeavors as it broadens the horizons of knowledge sharing. Literature with constrained, paid, or subscribed access imposes the limit on interdisciplinary studies and resourceful knowledge exploration. Open access facilitates collaborative learning and research in multidisciplinary areas. Smart grid research can serve as the best example of interdisciplinary and collaborative research outcome of the present era.

3. Improved Public Access and Engagement

Open research expedites and broadens the span of dissemination of facts and results. Some research results and investigations are of global public interest. For example, sharing of the research results conducted to find out adverse effects of the mobile phone as well as base station radiations is imperative to educate the citizens. Research in medical as well as paramedical fields plays a crucial role in information sharing and prevention of diseases.

4. Crossing the Barriers of Place, Time and Currency

The Internet is the most radical invention of present era as it ubiquitously and instantly serves the plethora of information beyond the constraints of time and place. Open research is beneficial for developing countries as they canaccess the most contemporary and cutting edge innovations of the developed countries without the barriers of place, time and currency. The major issue of affordability of literature subscription being faced by countries with weaker currencies can be resolved through open access.

5. Improved Education, Research, and Development

An education is inevitable for knowledge, survival, and growth. Information and communication technology has transformed the teaching-learning process but still, an education system is perceived as a tool to earn a certain qualification. An open research can expand and ignite the intellect of students beyond the four walls of classrooms and limited curriculum. Moreover, the qualities required for research and development can be instigated in the students at the early stage of education through open research. This can pave the path for students to build upon an existing knowledge.

6. Cross-Cultural Studies through Open Research

The universe can be observed in terms of profound diversities and cultural inequalities. In the present era, the world is facing challenges of multifaceted distinctiveness emerged due to complex dissimilarities in gender, culture, economy, and environment. Open research fosters rigorous study and transformative exchange between communities from diverse cultures and identities in the areas of science, arts, and humanities.

7. Covenant with Open Research/Access Directives

Creative common licenses foster legitimate and methodical sharing of the research documents. These licenses facilitate reuse, sharing, adaptation, modification, and distribution of creative work. An author can opt between CC BY, CC BY-SA, CC BY-ND, CC BY-NC-SA and CC BY-NC-ND licenses. CC-BY licenses are technologically extensive, uncomplicated, neutral and balanced as an issue of orphaned work is completely eradicated.

8. Bridging the Gap between Local and Global Research

Open research promotes universal sharing of findings through the World Wide Web. Dissemination of facts and findings can be achieved through self-archiving, institutional repositories, and open access journals. Open research eliminates the gap between local and universal research which arises especially in developing countries due to affordability and funding issues. Moreover, open research also fosters an integration between local and global research.

9. Open Research for Addressing Health, Environmental and Technological Issues

Several countries around the world are facing crucial issues pertaining to health and environment. Best practices can be adopted from dissemination of information through open research to address the issues related to health and ecology. Developing countries can be technologically uplifted through unobstructed access to research literature. The critical issues can be addressed through the dissemination of research results to various stakeholders such as policymakers, researchers, students, and masses.

10. Open Research for Eradication of Poverty and Malnutrition

Open research significantly influences living of people and aids to make this world a better place. Prof. Mary Abukutsa-Onyango has identified six nutritious African vegetables that can be grown in local weather conditions in a home garden [2]. Dissemination of this kind of research can be a boon to eradicate malnourishment and poverty in African countries.

11. Open Research for Grassroots

The Society for Research and Initiatives for Sustainable Technologies and Institutions (SRISTI) [3] is an example of open research for Grassroots in India. This organization fosters conservation of biodiversity and culture through research and innovations. The contributors of this research organization include students, teachers, scientists, farmers, clay craftsman and physically challenged person. This organization has transformed the perspective of research in the society as some of the innovations are accomplished by amateur, unschooled, and unaided researchers.

12. Open Research and Government Funding

Government-funded research must be made publicly available for the service of the community. The research grants of government-funded research projects are provided through taxes from citizens and thus dissemination of such research results is the greatest onus of giving back to society. Open research is inevitable for evolution and sustainability. Dissemination of information beyond social, financial, educational, and geographical barriers is essential for progression of humanity. Dissemination of knowledge through open research leads towards the greatest sense of gratification and sustainable development of civilisation.

References

1. Wang, X.; Liu, C.; Mao, W.; Fang, Z. The open access advantage considering citation, article usage and social media. *Scientometrics* **2015**, *103*, 555. [CrossRef]
2. Musotsi, A.A.; Sigot, A.J.; Onyango, M.O.A. The Role of Home Gardening in Household Food Security in Butere Division of Western Kenya. *AJFAND* **2008**, *8*, 375–390. [CrossRef]
3. Society for Research and Initiatives for Sustainable Technologies and Institutions (SRISTI). Available online: http://www.sristi.org/cms (accessed on 31 August 2018).

21 The Impact of Traditional vs Open Access on Scientific Publications

Miquesias Lopes-Pacheco

Over the last years, the amount of data and knowledge generated by the scientific community has sharply increased, requiring novel methods to more efficiently communicate and propagate the discoveries. In this line, open access research has broken barriers and brought several benefits compared to the traditional and subscription-based system, including: enhanced interdisciplinary conversation and wider collaboration between research groups, faster impact on the scientific community, greater visibility and transparency, and engagement of the non-scientific public.

Establishing reliable collaborations between research groups is an important step in achieving successful solutions. The dialogue between interdisciplinary researchers enables a broader overview about a certain issue with a higher number of possible approaches to test and validate hypotheses to solve it. Furthermore, open access research is usually cited earlier than content requiring subscription, which is an important altmetric in academia, and may faster stimulate the establishment of new collaborations that create networks on a global scale.

Most low- and middle-income countries have limited access of subscription-based publications, which prevents the fast dissemination of such advances in these populations. Open access to the most recent developments has helped these countries not only in dealing with practical priorities in diverse areas, such as public health, technology, and agriculture, but also provides a crucial starting point for developing their own research capacity. In fact, this is also extremely important for accelerating social and economic development in these regions.

Once a novel scientific content is available by open access, it can be promptly covered in the news and discussed in social media channels, thereby stimulating a widespread engagement. It also leads to an easier communication between the scientific and non-scientific public as well as a greater transparency on how the scientific budget has been used to bring solutions for issues and development that impact on the society in the short- and long-term. Moreover, patients and relatives' involvement in the research of certain health issues and in awareness events has become more noticeable. Open access has enabled those outside of research to directly benefit from new discoveries.

With the growing movement of integration induced by globalization, scientific research is also moving forward at an accelerated pace towards development for the society. Open access has become an important tool that offers greater equality and equity in the availability of scientific content worldwide.

22 Open Access Research: Bridging the Gap Towards Global Research Improvement

Jenichi Clairvaux Felizco

The Quacquarelli Symonds (QS) World University Rankings has recently released its most- anticipated annual list for 2018. Expectedly, Massachusetts Institute of Technology (MIT) has emerged on top, as it has consistently done for the sixth straight year now. MIT garnered an overall score of 100%, obtaining 99.9% for the criteria of citations per faculty. Needless to say, one key factor in maintaining a premiere university ranking for institutions such as MIT is by heavily investing in research. For the fiscal year 2016, it has reportedly totaled about $2.5 billion in expenditures for both sponsored and unsponsored research. This surely entails cutting-edge research facilities, complete academic journal subscriptions, the ability to conduct highly relevant research, and of course, increased capability to publish in academic journals. From the viewpoint of sustaining current research projects, more publications means more opportunities for research funding, and the cycle continues. This probably plays a big role in maintaining MIT's premiere ranking through the years. Way down the ranking list is University of the Philippines (UP), my undergraduate university, which ranked 367th this year. It has roughly 45,000 students, about four times that of MIT. Belonging to a developing country, UP has obviously much less research funds to dispose. For example, the total budget for research activities in 2014 for all state universities and colleges, where UP falls under, is about $20 million [1]. Only a small fraction of which, of course, is solely allocated to UP. Likewise, this shortage of research budget translates to a lack of research facilities, lower numbers of published papers, and insufficient funds for academic journal subscriptions. Putting issues of government budget allocations aside, there is one question that needs to be addressed—are there measures that can be undertaken in order to help lower-ranked universities bridge the gap towards improving the current state of their research?

Imagine a world of only open access journals. Surfing the internet probably feels like walking into a global library with an infinite number of free-to-use references. New knowledge is served fresh daily, with just a few clicks and a set of appropriate keywords, to anyone who wishes to get a taste. From professors to early career researchers to undergraduate students, the available resources from the most fundamental topics to the recent state-of-the art works can be readily accessed. From the researchers' perspective, open access research would remove the barrier from being updated in the recently published papers on their specific field. It will allow them not only to deepen their knowledge, but also to get fresh ideas for their own research. They get to look at their research from different points of view, something that paid access journals have restricted them from doing. This could inspire them to publish their own works. For authors, open access publication directly translates to greater exposure for their work, which is followed by higher number of citations. An increased author h-index usually paves the way for more research funding, which leads to more opportunities to expand the author's research, and more contributions to the research community. In addition, open access journals enable researchers from all over the world to be aware of the experiments that have already been tried or copyrighted. More often than not, unintentional replications of previously published methods occur as a result of lack of means to conduct intensive research. As a result, rejection of publication happens due to non-originality. Finally, there will not be a need for downloading subscription articles from illegal sites.

However, in reality, in order to enjoy the above-mentioned benefits of open access publication, one literally has to pay a hefty price. Nature Communications, for example, which is one of the top tier open access multidisciplinary journals with a 2016 impact factor of 12.124, charges about $5200 per article [2]. Naturally, only well-funded research groups are capable of publishing with such journals. As an indirect effect, some publishing companies are even stigmatized as utilizing extremely high open access article processing charges (APCs) as income-generating schemes. An ideal solution is to drive the article processing charges (APC) down to more affordable rates. Actually, there are publishing companies that offer open access publication at low APCs; but these journals have yet to improve on visibility and impact factor. But these can easily be overcome if researchers and publishers work hand-in-hand. Publishers can work harder on promoting affordable open access journals, in order to attract both readers and authors alike. Researchers, on the other hand, need to patronize these journals by reading and submitting to them, as well as citing their currently published papers. Through this, the true purpose of journal publication will be served—making new knowledge accessible to interested readers, regardless of financial status.

The key to globally improving the state of research is to allow lower-ranked universities to afford open access publication, as it is probably the best choice when it comes to showcasing one's new academic findings. It is important to keep in mind that new knowledge can emerge anytime and anywhere, irrespective of the level of sophistication of one's facilities. In this era of the Internet and automation, the capability to expose one's work to a wider audience has to be more of a right than a privilege. As Kurt Vonnegut puts it in his masterpiece *Breakfast of Champions*: "New knowledge is the most valuable commodity on earth. The more truth we have to work with, the richer we become".

References

1. Adriatico, C.; Yap, F.R. Research Budget Allocation of Higher Education in the Philippines: Use of Fractal Analysis. *JHERD* **2015**, *1*, 189–195. Available online: https://www.ijterm.org/index.php/jehrd/article/view/78/69s (accessed 10 October 2018).
2. Nature Communications. Article Processing Charges, 2018. Nature Communications. Available online: https://www.nature.com/ncomms/about/article-processing-charges (accessed 10 October 2018).

23 The Effects of Open Research on the Scientific World

Afrina Mustari

1. Introduction

Open research or open science is the term that can be well expressed as the dispersion of scientific knowledge openly as soon as it is practical in the invention process. It involves making overall research materials, data and lab procedures freely available online to everybody. Open research clarifies research techniques, such as making transparent the data and tools used in the research process by making them openly available. Open research enables scientists to use the ideas of the best research around the world through the results, protocols, data and all aspects of the research in the desired fields. These handy findings will increase research reproducibility, and will create a favorable environment in the scientific world.

2. Importance of Open Research

2.1. Benefits for Authors

Open research which is published in open access articles are viewed more often in comparison to articles that are only available to subscribers, and increase the chance for citation. Increased attraction to the public and subsequent engagement can occur, especially for research in which there is a strong public interest. Open research helps researchers to build collaborative research on a global scale. Open research meets funder requirements as well as quality for special funds. It helps them obtain funds for the continuation of published research or to set up a new protocol. Practitioners can use the findings of open research. In some cases the research can even influence implementation of policy or laws.

2.2. Benefits for the Articles

Through opening the articles, journals can accelerate the process of getting impact. The increased visibility by researchers creates a positive attitude among them to publish their work in open access journals. Open research increases interdisciplinary conversation though allowing judging of novel approaches to traditional problems. By sorting new inventions, open research can accelerate the pace of scientific enquiry.

3. Constraints of Restricted Research

Many researchers suffer from a lack of access to research protocols. Especially in the developing countries, researchers experience trouble to subscribe or to pay access fees. The public will be unable to get access to the research. Only some reputed university and educational institutions have access to restricted research, where services are free at the point of use for staff and students in learning, teaching and research through institutional subscriptions. On the other hand, the majority of them can't support their young researchers to obtain their desired research protocols or data. So the restricted research ultimately limits the utilization of skills for many promising scientists, and access to new innovation processes.

4. Global Impact of Open Research

Now is the age of scientific revolution. Scientific fields are becoming closer to each other, leading to the discovery of new technology by overlapping different disciplines. Open research can be favorable in helping this approach. Nowadays researchers want to collaborate with other disciplines to utilize the best technology. Open science enhances the scope such opportunities. Today, scientific research relies more and more heavily on computer codes and software for simulations, analysis, calculations, visualization and signal or data processing, so it's important to have access to those codes and software. Moreover, it's essential to publish inventions so that the results can be repeated and validated. The said results also improve the transfer of knowledge from academia to industry. Many research institutes have potential researchers who can contribute to the scientific world but due to lack of proper knowledge about previous work in the similar discipline they can't obtain enough funds. Scientists from developing countries lack modern technology although they have a keen interest to make new discoveries. In this case, they can communicate with famous scientists though open research, thus engaging themselves in the innovation process. Sometimes scientists need to write anew research project, but if they can't get access to previous research it is quite tough to overview the writing. Practicing open science can improve research practices and increase study reliability. If scientists share their obtained materials and data, other scientists can more easily evaluate them, so it increases the quality of the research. By sharing their materials and data, scientists create scope for others to use and analyze them in new ways, potentially leading to new discoveries, thus speeding up scientific discovery.

5. Traditional Belief Lies behind Open Research

Researchers have been practicing closed science for years, even decades, and changing these old habits requires some more motivation. Some researchers think that others will steal their ideas and publish first if they disclose their findings. But these conventional habits need to be motivated to change to a more positive way. In fact, open research protects the researcher and restricts the chance of duplication. Open research makes scientists even more popular among the scientific community. If the researcher opens his technology a scientist from the same field may get involved in the different technology and ultimately this practice will reduce the duplication of effort and will be economically cost effective. On the other hand, with greater access to information through open research, more people working separately on the same problems can solve them more efficiently and with greatest transparency. In the present times, if the research remains closed it may lead to errors that are more difficult to highlight without full sharing of procedures, data and publications.

24   Open Sesame!

Magaret Sivapragasam

"Open Sesame!" yelled Ali Baba. He then made his way meticulously into the secret cave and took a bag of gold coins home to his family. This is a snippet from the legendary tale of Ali Baba and the forty thieves which was narrated by Antoine Galland in the 18th century. Imagine the amount of "gold" the world we would be able to reap if research were made open and free!

During the First Annual Address to Congress in 8 January 1790, former President of the United States George Washington mentioned, "There is nothing which can better deserve your patronage, than the promotion of science and literature. Knowledge is in every country the surest basis of public happiness". This was a resonating quote from the great George Washington on the importance of science and technology and he has since established a quote that endured centuries.

I am a postdoctoral research scientist working on ecotoxicological risk assessments of ionic liquids in Malaysia. My day-to-day life includes a lot of reading and analysing manuscripts to keep myself abreast with the current knowledge and trends in my field. I greatly rely on open research so that I can access these scientific platforms from anywhere I am. Open access databases have been my best friend even when I am away from my institution. The freedom it gives me to be able to access literature from wherever I am located has certainly been a high! It can only be my hope that one day all research materials are made free and accessible to the public wherever they may be. These are my views on the global benefits of open research.

The idea of open research is to provide a platform designed to make scientific processes and results transparent while making it accessible to people outside the research niche. This includes making research materials and data freely available online to the public. However, debates surrounding open research have garnered much attention from many viewpoints and some say that these views are multifaceted. There is a definite lack of consensus regarding open research. I, as a scientist, firmly believe that openly disseminating knowledge in science will reap benefits. The benefactors include students, researchers, industries, developing countries, entrepreneurs and publishers.

Firstly, open research will increase greater public engagement in science. By making it accessible, scientific information is available to those who cannot access subscription content. This also includes new and young universities which may not have the access to funds or revenue to pay for subscription fees. Due to the confounding price of journal subscriptions, even most well-funded institutions cannot provide their students with the complete scholarly record of all publication houses. Sadly, students at smaller colleges and universities must make do with their limited access to this scholarly information. Ironically, once their tenure at an institution is over, so is the access to these portals.

Without access to the latest data, the research and development industries cannot harness the latest scientific information that could potentially drive new areas of the economy. This would be particularly in industries who rely on up-to-date information to yoke new products and technology. On another note, science should be open for the whole society, so it may promote awareness among citizens. Access to journals is a major barrier for people in developing countries. With proper access to the latest ground-breaking research, citizens—especially in developing countries—may increase their general knowledge. This may also give rise to societies with a greater sense of intellect, which could in turn help to build trust and support for the generation of public policies and investments.

Open access articles are viewed and cited more often than paid articles, without a doubt. This, in turn, leads to an increased citation of that manuscript. Authors can be much more visible, and their area of study made to be more prominent. More discovery leads to more citations and mentions, and this leads to higher academic reputation and higher chances of potential funding and collaborators. New findings and ideas can be disseminated quickly, which serves as an impetus for knowledge.

Greater access to scientific inputs and outputs can improve the effectiveness and productivity of the research system. This may reduce duplication of data or "fake science". When a manuscript is published, the author is then aware that the manuscript is available freely for the entire world to see, which would create an awareness that they need to provide data as accurately as possible and without falsification. This will also inevitably reduce the hacking of manuscripts online through free hacking software.

Science has indeed sparked monumental advances in today's world. Without a doubt, fundamental and advanced research will be a pioneer to sustain the upcoming generations. Open science is inevitably worldwide, and we must take advantage of it. It can encourage collaborative efforts and is an incentive for knowledge transfer for a better understanding of challenges that require global actions, such as the issue of climate change. However, open research remains one of the numerous trials that the scholarly publishing system is facing.

There are always two sides to a coin. I choose to see open research as a beneficial win–win situation. What do you say?

25 The Global Benefits of Open Research and How It Can Change Scientific Publishing

Bernhard C. Geiger

Research can only be open if its results are. Studies have shown that Open Access publications tend to get cited [1] more [2] often [3]; admit implementing research findings faster, which is particularly important in healthcare [4]; and reduce the time between research and the introduction of new products and services [5]. Aside from that, Open Access facilitates greater knowledge transfer to low-income countries, thus contributing to greater knowledge equity.

Open Research also embraces the principles of Open Data, Open Notebooks, and Open Source, i.e., the aim to make materials and methods used for research publicly available. Society and academia are not required to believe research results in good faith but are given the tools to reproduce them, making it possible to carefully check every step and to question every implicit assumption. This makes science as a whole more trustworthy and accelerates scientific progress. A prime example is the fast-paced development of Deep Learning: Academic source code made available by authors, open source software packages such as Tensorflow [6], Open data such as ImageNet [7], the MNIST database [8], or the UCI Machine Learning Repository [9] allow fellow researchers and interested laypersons to inspect algorithms, implement new ideas effortlessly, and incrementally and quickly advance the state of the art.

But Open Research goes even further. Rather than just making it easy to reproduce, Open Research makes it easy to participate. Laypersons and researchers from all over the world are invited to join efforts to solve a research problem. The result, the data, and the method become open to the public—and so does the process of "getting there". Open Research thus not only accelerates progress by faster incremental improvements, but has the unique potential to advance science in directions that would otherwise not be pursued: If a researcher has an idea but lacks the required skills, then the idea will not be implemented. Open Research can bring together those with ideas and those with skills more efficiently than any classic scientific collaboration could, in a framework less bureaucratic than any government—or industry-funded project. A recent example of success is the development of an enantiopure version of a drug for a parasitic infection called schistosomiasis [10]. A pill made of this drug would be smaller, less bitter, and would have fewer side effects, which would be a relief for the hundreds of millions of people affected by schistosomiasis worldwide.

Open Research projects are never finished. At any time, a research group may decide to throw in ideas or work on the current methods to improve the results. This, in turn, has the potential to fundamentally change scientific publishing, beyond continuing the trend towards Open Access. On the one hand, results from the project can be published in progress reports. This admits continued use of traditional publication venues, but may speed up the cycle in which publications are written, published, and become obsolete. On the other hand, though, the project consortium may decide to publish with the aim of informing the world about the state of the art. The publication then needs to change in sync with the results, something that is hardly compatible with today's prevalent publication practices. Indeed, only a few repositories (e.g., arXiv) and publishers (e.g., F1000Research) allow updating of documents while simultaneously keeping track of previous versions. Perhaps the future will tell that the best way to publish is a Wiki, the quality of which is ensured via replacing classical peer review by an open, moderated discussion.

Admittedly, the last paragraph hints at a potential future not everyone will welcome—current, traditional publishers surely will not. Aside from that, however, the benefits of Open Research—truly open collaborations, faster incremental improvements of the state of the art, opening the possibility to pursue new research directions, faster and stronger transfer of knowledge, greater equity in education—are indisputable. But benefits for science are benefits for everyone: As Steven Pinker recently wrote, we live longer, work less, fight less wars, fewer of us are poor, and more of us live in democracies. We owe this to replacing "superstition and magic with science" [11]. What better motivation is there to make research open?

References

1. OpCit Project. The Effect of Open Access and Downloads ('Hits') on Citation Impact: A Bibliography of Studies, 2004; 2013. OpCit Project. Available online: http://opcit.eprints.org/oacitation-biblio.html (accessed on 12 September 2018).
2. Jump, P. Open Access Papers 'Gain More Traffic and Citations'. *Times Higher Education*, 30 July 2014 . Available online: https://www.timeshighereducation.com/home/open-access-papers-gain-more-traffic-and-citations/2014850.article (accessed on 12 September 2018).
3. MacCallum, C.J.; Parthasarathy, H. Open Access Increases Citation Rate. *PloS* **2006**, *4*, e176. Available online: https://journals.plos.org/plosbiology/article?id=10.1371/journal.pbio.0040176(accessed on 12 September 2018).

4.   Anderson, T. 6 Reasons Open Access Matters to the Medical Community, 2011. The Right to Research Coalition. Available online: http://www.righttoresearch.org/blog/6-reasons-open-access-matters-to-the-medical-commu.shtml (accessed on 12 September 2018).

5.   Foster.   What Are the Benefits of Open Science?   Available online: https: //www.fosteropenscience.eu/content/what-are-benefits-open-science   (accessed   on 10 February 2018).

6.   Tensorflow. Available online: https://www.tensorflow.org/ (accessed on 12 September 2018).

7.   ImageNet. Available online: http://www.image-net.org/ (accessed on 12 September 2018).

8.   MNIST database. Available online: http://yann.lecun.com/exdb/mnist/ (accessed on 12 September 2018)C.

9.   UCI Machine Learning Repository. Available online: https://archive.ics.uci.edu/ml/datasets.html (accessed on 12 September 2018).

10.   Woelfle, M.; Piero, O.; Todd, M.H. Open Science Is A Research Accelerator. *Nature Chemistry* **2011**, *3*, 745–748. Available online: https://www.nature.com/articles/nchem.1149 (accessed on 10 February 2018).

11.   Pinker, S. The Enlightenment Is Working. *The Wall Street Journal*. 9 February 2018. Available online: www.wsj.com/articles/the-enlightenment-is-working-1518191343 (accessed on 10 February 2018).

26 The Academic, Industrial and Societal Impacts of Open Research

Fitya Syarifa Mozar

Nowadays, open research practice has garnered massive attention from various academic and research institutions globally. Open research has become more mainstream ever since web-based platform such as Figshare and Researchgate continued to grow in term of users and research output numbers. The term 'open research' itself means conducting research within free and open source platforms, where transparency and openness of scientific information sharing are the main principles. The purposes of this practice are to provide open access scientific information as well as enhance collaboration and engagement with wider audiences.

While open research deviates from traditional research secrecy habits, its application is necessary in this increasingly globalized world. Everything is connected via the Internet and things move more rapidly now compared to former times due to more advanced technology. Therefore, in order to keep up with this fast-moving and high demand world, faster application of research discovery in various sectors is required. One example is in the medical research field. A massive growth in human populations and higher life expectancy has created a jump in disease incidences worldwide. The most common one is cancer, a highly complex and multifactorial disease which is very difficult to eradicate. If there is only one research team working on it, the progress will be very slow. Open research practice allows methodological and data sharing, enabling teams all over the world to build on previous findings and even test them on multiple types of cancer at once. This way, formulations of new cancer treatments would become much faster. Multidisciplinary collaborations among different specializations could also be achieved, creating more holistic approaches. As a result, the transition from preclinical to clinical studies will be easier, since wider research coverage will make the data more convincing and conclusive. Early and successful clinical trials increase the possibility of mass production, which in turn would be beneficial for patients and the pharmaceutical industry.

Not only consumers or patients, but also the researchers themselves get advantages from open research practice. Increased visibility, citation rates and discoverability of their publications will lift the researcher's reputations internationally, therefore enhancing their chance for job promotions as well as funding opportunities. Researchers in developing countries, who might not have enough funding to subscribe to high impact journals can also participate and contribute to the project. Starting from 2017, many organizations such as the Wellcome Trust, Medical Research Council (MRC) and National Institutes of Health (NIH) accept preprint submissions for grant applications. Moreover, in the same year, the European Commission published guidelines entitled "Evaluation of Research Careers fully acknowledging Open Science Practices" [1], indicating increased demand for open research in science community worldwide. Soon, reproducibility and open science will become standard practice and hold a more important role for scientist career advancement.

The impact of open research could also be felt by the wider community, given that much taxpayer money is used to fund government research grant. The public health field is one of the key areas in community-based research, where the implementation of multi-sectoral public policies is one of its objectives. Open research practice could easily influence policymaker's decision-making processes due to faster online data sharing and accessibility. This could be highly beneficial during a disease outbreak, which requires faster intervention.

In fact, open research is not a totally new thing in science, technology, engineering and mathematics (STEM). Platforms such as arXiv and bioRxiv have already existed for several years, providing preprint sharing options in topics including physics, mathematics and computer science. Feedback from other readers could help improve manuscript quality and also ensure originality of the research ideas. Additionally, digital object identifiers (DOI) assigned to each manuscript would facilitate citation of preprints, even before the peer review process.

I think it is important to integrate science in daily life, where citizens could participate and produce their own research project. Web-based service such as Crowdcrafting open the opportunity for citizens to contribute intellectually to others' research projects, share resources and opinions, even starting their own projects. All services are 100% free, permitting people from various backgrounds to join. By bringing science to people, we could encourage critical thinking and an innovative mentality in young generations.

Last but not least, industry participation is a key link for research promotion and mass production. In order to manage research data at industrial scales, big data analysis skills hold a vital role. Besides, legal issues involving Intellectual Property (IP), licensing agreements, and state policies also should be taken into account from the beginning of collaborations between scientists and industry. Those abovementioned data science and science policy fields will be desirable career alternatives for STEM graduates with the growing importance of open science.

A number of tech giants such as Google, Apple, Samsung, Microsoft etc. are starting to use open science approaches in their research and development (R & D), and business models. Fast and agile innovations are required if they want to stay on top, since competitors arise all the time. Massive research collaborations of industries, academia, and corporation partners have led to many technological breakthroughs, enabling their brands to flourish in the market. The latest trend is the race for Artificial Intelligence (AI) apps, hence many brands have set up AI labs in various countries, most notably Canada. Amazingly, local professors and students are also invited to develop the algorithms in joint AI research with industry. Consequently, new technology upgrades more rapidly, every year new AI models with better specifications are produced. This speed is only made possible through open research collaborations. When costumers are satisfied with the product, companies' revenue will increase; thus higher funding could be allocated for R & D activities.

To put it briefly, open research practice has clearly proven to be beneficial for all sectors of society. It is time to prioritize collective science advancement, not only individual interest in scientific research. Mindset revolution in academia is a must in this increasingly globalized world. By developing standardized guidelines, hopefully the transition to open research will be smoother for scientists worldwide.

References

1. European Commission. Evaluation of Research Careers fully acknowledging Open Science Practices. Rewards, Incentives and/or Recognition for Researchers Practicing Open Science. Publications Office of the European Union: Luxembourg, 2017. Available online: https://ec.europa.eu/research/openscience/pdf/os_rewards_wgreport_final.pdf (accessed on 11 September 2018).

27   Global Consequences of Open Research

Ravi Sahu and Manisha Hariram

Research benefits everyone globally, and in an ideal world, findings would be readily available to everyone anywhere in the world. But the truth is that only a limited number of research works are accessible to all, especially the works that are publicly funded. Approximately 700 open access policies and mandates have been recorded globally from a range of research institutes and funding bodies (roarmap.eprints.org). Although its benefits are becoming more popular, nowadays progress is rather slow. Advancement in any research field is necessary for it to fulfill its purpose. More precisely, one should not knowingly waste time in repeating the same research that has been attempted elsewhere just because the information on it was not accessible. Therefore, open study provides a forum for others to access the previous research in the field and let others work further ahead. Further, to others, it may provide essential information relevant to the topic of their interests. As a whole, open research benefits people globally.

Open access research refers to no access charges, unhindered online access to research outputs, such as journal articles, books, etc. It removes obstacles to accessing, sharing and re-using the results of scholarly investigations, and fosters a tradition of more substantial scientific literacy. The underlying principle is that research progress is facilitated by certifying swift and extensive access to findings, such that the public at the global level has the prospect to build upon them. It has broader benefits to research through improved visibility, facilitating access to the latest research status of a particular field, and decreasing financial pressures on academic libraries. It helps to promote clear, high-quality prose that powerfully communicates vital scientific concepts without any obstructions. It deals with greater public engagement due to its open access nature to everyone.

In the case of students, it may present a platform to update their knowledge in any field. Through the latest research, a complete education in their field of study, students may hit the ground running after graduation. As far as researchers are concerned, their effort is useless if it's not shared with others, making it ineffectual if others aren't able to go through it and build on it. In other words, if access barriers keep articles locked away, science cannot achieve its full potential.

Studies have shown a significant augmentation in citations when articles are made openly accessible. Increased citation and usage and faster impact can be achieved provided that the research is made open. Furthermore, there is a higher chance of citation and feasibility for work, as it can enhance the interdisciplinary applicability and broaden collaborations. The Human Genome Project can be cited as an example of the ability of open access to transform publications and data to a more fabulous resource for innovation. This international, collaborative research project was facilitated by the use of open data, with all the gene sequence data made openly available for everyone to reuse.

The only issue that remains with open access is that publishing may not be affordable for any single individual or research group. A significant reason behind this issue is that even for those in a privileged position, institutes do not always provide authors with the funds to cover open access journals' processing charges. There is a need to understand that subscriptions to access articles is not even required if the articles are openly available online. Further, many less reputed journals in search of increasing their business do make articles open access but are not peer-reviewed. This can lead to a negative image of open access journals with academics. Consequently, the potential impact of even the best research is never fully realized, impeding scientific advancement by a lack of application, while simultaneously negatively affecting the credit of individual researchers.

Therefore, from academic, economic, and societal perspectives, open research or open access seeks to return scholarly publishing to its original intent. Numerous articles have revealed that open access research articles are viewed more frequently compared to materials that are only accessible to particular subscribers. Indeed, they are cited more often as well in comparison. Being responsible researchers, authors should genuinely understand its crucial role in making their research works more accessible, not only to a group of researchers in their field of interest, but a broader readership. The extensive analysis allows students, researchers, publishers, entrepreneurs, stakeholders, doctors, patients and the wider public to explore published work in more detail. It does justice to the efforts that authors put in to add knowledge to the existing information in any particular field.

In short, open research helps to spread awareness and allow that knowledge to be built upon. Public availability of scholarly research may cause a significant positive impact on everything from improvement in the practice of medicine to the knack of entrepreneurs to innovate. Open access can ensure students acquire the best learning and are not falsely restricted by the choice of scholarly journals their institutes can afford. On the other hand, limited access to research makes scholars settle for the information that is presented rather than that which is most relevant. Overall, open investigation encourages people globally to gain existing knowledge in already explored fields and let others develop it more rapidly without putting up barriers to access.

28   Drawing an Accessible Future for New Generations

Michael Nones

Thinking of the benefits of open science and sharing of research data, two main thoughts arise to me: on the one side, my newborn; on the other side, the country that I left to continue my studies. Probably the former is worse, since in Italy, as in other countries, there is a growing mass movement of no-vax, which bases its "knowledge" on reading news on the internet, without taking care of the source. As any researcher knows, vaccines are necessary to protect society as a whole, especially the new generations, and therefore, despite very few cases of vax-related issues, it makes no sense to be against vaccination based on a mere belief it can hurt. In my mind, free access to better science and sharing of research outcomes could be a boost in changing the minds of people who usually do not read scientific articles and reports (provided they are able to understand them, which is an issue I do not want to discuss further here). Given the wider spread of the internet, open research and sharing of data by means of different media mean the improvement for all parties, regardless of their instruction level and background.

As for my baby, he has just turned eleven months and grows day by day full of enthusiasm and surprise. For the future, I would like to see him, and all the other babies around the world, gain new knowledge based on the most up-to-date discoveries. At the present stage, however, the diffusion of science is uneven, since paying access to articles and data affects their availability and dissemination, preventing the opportunity for low-income countries or specific parties in obtaining new information and potentially contributing to the improvement of the subject.

Among open data issues, I think the availability of good as well as bad results (especially bad unpublished) would help deepen understanding of processes and address lack of information. In science every attempt is worth doing, provided the validity and significance of the assumptions on which it is based. Therefore, having a database of fails, in most disciplines, with some metadata describing the main possible reasons for the occurred problems, would be a great benefit to avoid similar failing results and boost the overall productivity (because science is slowly becoming like an industry, in all its fields, with information only rarely travelling the globe and addressing the right parties).

Moreover, cutting-edge research needs funding, and it makes very little sense to concentrate most of it in literature review rather than in doing science. Especially in countries were few public funds are available (e.g., in Europe, Spain and again Italy), and private companies do not (yet) effectively support science-related research, having free access to state of the art research would enhance good quality research, allowing an effective investment of the available funds.

Open science also means to broaden the view to a world that can be explained in detail, which is scary only if people do not want explanations but prefer to believe their own thoughts (as in the no-vax issue already mentioned). If you had some history classes: In the Middle Ages there was closed access to knowledge, and the permitted and available knowledge was cloistered and scrutinised. The tendency to base every aspect of life on belief and the fear to act differently from what was thought correct was the leading view. Through science, Middle Ages Europe evolved; the first universities were founded and a re-birth period (the Renaissance) started, boosting movement of people around Europe. If we want to stop that, then closed access is the right way. The media have to simplify things to make information mass-explicit, but comprehension comes not from summaries, but rather from combining important self-organised concepts from different sources, which should be freely available for interested parties.

Lastly, to return to my child's future, it is unbelievable how much a little human being learns by doing, and by watching others doing. At a certain point his own abilities are not sufficient to keep on track if he is not provided with an effective support. "Surfing the web" will be much easier for our children that it has been for us, and making sense of the huge amount of information available is not always easy. We have learned with books and encyclopedia that they will use the web. How to filter good and reliable information from bad sources, especially on science, if most of it is just enclosed in academia?

A growing movement towards open research and free sharing of data and research outcomes can contribute to overcome such issues. But a real change in the university system and researchers' minds is necessary, since presently academics are more focused on their own world, keeping results private to push their publications and increase the h-index. More collaborative methods and sharing of data among all possible interested parties is the only key to increase our knowledge, and guarantee a better world for our children.

29 The Impact of Open Access on Global Challenges Research

Paula Fraga-Lamas

We have made incredible leaps of knowledge as humankind. Open research plays a decisive role in allowing us to fulfil the mission of advancing worldwide knowledge. Its core idea grounds its key advantage: democratization of knowledge. Research is freely available online for anyone in the whole world who wishes to access and share it in order to confront global challenges.

Specifically, open access publication makes research permanently accessible without restriction, which can grant benefits to all the stakeholders in the process: students, librarians, authors, business developers, funders, researchers, publishers, the general public, and society as a whole. The different stakeholders benefit from open research in different ways. For example, for students and libraries/archives, the benefits of avoiding the payment for individual articles, books or journal subscriptions are noticeable.

We cannot forget that the costs of publication are frequently the responsibility of the author, perhaps through their employer or a research grant. In times of funding cuts, these costs may hamper researchers who want to publish open access. But, depending on the journal, open publishing can have the same fees or less than traditional publishing.

As a senior researcher, I am fully aware of the pros of open research. Authors can take advantage of the unrestricted availability of their research to others, potentially leading to a rise in the prominence and usage of their work. In an era where the number of published documents is skyrocketing, the utilization of open access approaches can ease the discoverability of an article or result. Ultimately, a large amount of readers can be converted into citations for the author, mentions in media and social media, higher credits (e.g., references to data), extra funding (e.g., rewards, awards), reuse of datasets, prevention of duplicate works or improved networking (e.g., new job opportunities, promotion, tenure or better workload distribution).

Open research can often be utilized without the need to request additional authorization from publishers. For example, an article could be included in a presentation or a university course package, or even translated into a different language. Accordingly, it is possible to enable anyone to make derivative versions of an open access manuscript or outcome (note that this will depend upon the particular Creative Commons license applied).

Researchers can access scientific literature anywhere, even outside the university, without encountering paywalls or subscription options. In developing and low income countries, the non-access to journals is a common claim of the researchers. Global open research can trigger collective empowerment and equality, providing scientists in such countries with the chance to belong to an international research community. Today, some publications offer discounted or waived publication fees for papers coming from low-income countries.

Furthermore, the outcomes of research programs are becoming free to society, to ensure enhanced transparency of the use of public funding. For instance, many funding bodies like the European Commission have encouraged or mandated open research due to its potential for a greater return on investment. Open research for the whole of society promotes awareness among citizens, evidencing the outcomes of public funded research, and helps to build trust and endorsement for public policies. Besides, it encourages citizen engagement and active involvement in scientific experimentation, research trials and data collection (e.g., smart city crowdsourcing). As a result, open research means access for society at large and potentially greater public engagement with the significance of science and technology. Furthermore, open research can help workers outside academia (e.g., teachers, lawyers or even business developers) who rely on research, to profit from the retrieval of the latest key findings.

Besides, open access publications and open source tools (e.g., GitHub) are enablers to help researchers to undertake collaborative work on an international scale, increasing the ability to create research networks. For example, open access journals with interdisciplinary approaches can help researchers with a different background to connect more easily.

Whilst not an issue for reputable, renowned and trustworthy publishers, some people could argue that the utilization of open access models incentivize the publication of articles. Publishers have to face their operating costs, and their revenue business model comes largely from publication fees. Nevertheless, to ensure the sustainability of the system, publishers should be encouraged to publish articles that guarantee excellence in aspects like novelty, significance, quality of presentation or scientific soundness.

Wider access to scientific inputs and outputs can evolve the effectiveness and productivity of the research system, by lowering the costs of creating and transferring—multiplying opportunities for global involvement in the research process. Open access to scientific datasets and other outputs that assist the research process raises the opportunity for inspection by the scientific community, thus allowing for more accurate validation, replication and improvement of the results. This examination enables self-correction principles, allowing for prompt identification of any misconduct, fraud or human errors, and therefore it is straightforward to detect or eliminate these practices for the benefit of scientific integrity.

Ubiquitous access to research outcomes can foster spillovers, not only to science, but also to knowledge and technology transfer in innovation systems, as well as increase conscious choices among citizens. Science plays a strategic role in the competitiveness of economies, and the higher efficiency associated to open research would benefit both advanced and developing economies. Furthermore, open research and innovation can reduce delays in the reuse of the results of research, and promote the shortest path from research to technology and knowledge transfer; and innovation to produce disruptive products and services.

The value of open research extends to the whole of society. Research is inevitably global and it must take advantage of it. It can foster innovation, create economic growth, endorse collaboration and speed up knowledge and technology transfer for a holistic comprehension of the societal challenges that require coordinated actions, such as war refugees and immigration, climate change, cancer, chronic diseases, supply chain traceability, transparency, corruption, inequality or the ageing population, and could help to uncover solutions more effectively. Finally, one motto for the researchers: Keep your rights, decide how your research work is used, face global challenges and advance society!

30   Why Care About the Higgs Boson

Spiros Kitsinelis

There are cases where the benefit of a discovery is clear and direct. A few years ago the Nobel Prize for Chemistry went to people that worked on computer models describing how large molecules such as proteins behave and react [1]. Everyone understands that this can lead to easier drug design. The same goes for the Nobel Prize for Medicine of the same year [2]. Understanding cell communication mechanisms can lead to faster treatments of various diseases.

On the other hand, a discovery in particle physics can be of paramount importance because it tells us that the model we have of the cosmos still holds but it is not clear where it could lead us. For example, we verified the existence of the Higgs boson and thus the Higgs field that gives mass to other particles that scientists predicted years ago. The general public, citizens whose taxes are used for such research, will often wonder about the big fuss and why such projects are being funded when there are so many other pressing everyday problems to deal with. The truth is that we cannot know the effects of such discoveries and it may be many years before we realize the actual impact and any dramatic changes in our lives.

From astronomical observations, important theories were developed that describe the gravity of bodies and centuries later we had the theories of relativity. Humanity built on that knowledge and several decades later we had technologies that gave us our satellites, the GPS and the ability to send scientific instruments to other worlds. We also had observations of atomic properties that led to quantum theory and decades later we had lasers and computers. But how can the non-specialist contemporary of Newton, Einstein and Planck know how important all these things are and where they will lead ... Even for the experts it is very difficult to predict the impact of all that we constantly discover.

My message is that it is not necessary for the practical impact to be immediate in order for the discovery to be important. Anything that reveals how the world works is important on both a philosophical and a technological level. We can always talk about our deep need as a species to explore and answer questions but history has also shown us that basic research leads to significant practical outcomes that improve our lives considerably sooner or later.

And for the reader that enjoys finding articles online, surfing the internet and exploring cyberspace, I have this final comment: In order to find if the Higgs boson exists, we built the largest particle accelerator at CERN . . . and it was there that the World Wide Web of the Internet was developed.

References

1. The Nobel Prize in Chemistry 2013. The Nobel Prize. Available online: https://www.nobelprize.org/prizes/chemistry/2013/summary/ (accessed on 11 September 2018).
2. The Nobel Prize in Physiology or Medicine 2013. The Nobel Prize. Available online: https://www.nobelprize.org/prizes/medicine/2013/summary/ (accessed on 11 September 2018).

31   Open Research: What's More?

Stefano Cinti

To highlight the benefits of open research, everyone should understand what "research" means. Before discussing the relevance of a certain way to communicate scientific achievements, everyone needs to know that the meaning of the word "research" is both sharing and improving knowledge. The figure of a researcher is not fully understood: at least in Italy, the amount of people who do not know what a researcher does during his/her working day is (unfortunately) huge. Prior to carrying out new experiments or prior to writing a new drama essay, the researcher needs to read. Read what? In order to improve the actual knowledge regarding a specific field, i.e., medicine, chemistry, arts, etc., the researcher should be updated about the existing "literature" in that field. The literature is full of a plethora of documents that help researchers worldwide make their research activities useful, perhaps without performing studies that have been already carried out by someone else. At the end, if valuable, the research will be published and, depending on its relevance and ambition, it will be published as a book, an article or video, etc. All these documents are stored in many databases. An author can decide to publish her/his findings in so-called "open access" sources: this means that everybody can access the results of scholarly research. Why should a journal need to be defined as "open"? Because, nowadays, most of the published documents are not open. Consequently, this means that if someone wants to read that paper, that person needs to pay for it. In the past, I have asked myself "why would my father, who is a retired railway worker, be interested about the synthesis of a new compound?" This question can be simply answered: he wants to improve his knowledge. However, an author that is interested in publishing open access documents usually encounters the article processing charge, while most of the journals which are not open access allow the authors to publish free of charge (but the readers pay). Even if the cost associated to publish on open access platforms might discourage researchers, the benefits of open research affect both the research community and society.

From a reader's point of view: no payment is needed, which means that all the researchers that cannot usually access a specific journal, are now able to read all the documents if the research is open. There are many financially-restricted universities which cannot afford the payment to access a needed source. This issue limits the work of the researchers of that institution. Open research represents a clear step forward for them.

From the author's point of view: by choosing an open access platform, the visibility of a published research article will increase. This has been reported by several studies that have demonstrated how open access content attracts more attention than non-open access content. The visibility is strictly correlated with the possibility of increasing the importance of that research article and subsequently to benefit the author's career. In fact, one of the important parameters that is used to evaluate the importance of a paper is the amount of citations: if everyone can read a paper, the paper will have a higher possibility of being cited. Studies have shown that open access articles are viewed more often than articles that are only available to subscribers and are cited more often.

From a collaborative point of view: the opening of publications and data enables researchers to perform collaborative research worldwide. The Human Genome Project (1990–2003), an international research program aimed to complete the mapping and understanding of all the genes of human beings, represents a clear evidence of the benefits of open research. The access to publications and data allowed this project to be a much more powerful resource for research, education and innovation.

From an educational point of view: all the open access works can often be re-used to educate students. For instance, by creating brand-new derivative documents that are capable of impassioning students, by catching their attention and enhancing their understanding. The benefits of open research strongly affect teachers: these open platforms allow them to always use more accurate examples to explain concepts.

From the public engagement point of view: do you remember my father, and his necessity to read about research findings? Without open research, he would not have been informed about the impact of the Fukushima nuclear accident on the humans and nature. The impact of making research items freely accessible from the moment of publication can be astonishing, particularly for research in which there is a strong public interest.

Open research is establishing itself as a fundamental tool for many purposes: from academia to public engagement, everyone can access the new findings, improving their knowledge and participation.

32 Open Research: Much Ado About Nothing?

Tochukwu Ozulumba

Recent developments have seen intensified calls for a more open research culture in science. Changing the status quo in a field notorious for its elitist and secretive nature may appear daunting at first but promises long-term benefits for all.

Open research is principled on a transparent approach to scientific investigations, honest public engagement, and free access to scholarly publications, datasets and research tools such as software and protocols. Fuelled by the rising popularity of the Internet, the open access movement was birthed in the 1990s as a response to growing dissatisfaction with traditional subscription-based publishing models [1]. Elimination of paywalls means that all scientists, irrespective of location or affiliation, can have equal access to high quality journal articles. Since the publication of the first commercial open access journal, *BioMed Central*, in 1998, the field has witnessed significant growth with over 11,000 journals currently indexed in the Directory of Open Access Journals. Publishing open access offers authors the advantages of a transparent peer review process, increased citations and visibility, higher public engagement, and autonomy over rights retention and reuse [2]. It also supports the view that research funded with taxpayers' monies should be publicly accessible.

Sharing research protocols, data and software can foster interdisciplinary collaborations and improve scientific productivity. Connecting researchers from diverse backgrounds and expertise can provide faster routes for tackling complex scientific challenges. A prime example is the Human Genome Project which comprised twenty universities and research centres from six countries. Having sequence data publicly available facilitated timely completion, 2 years ahead of schedule. Making the Protein Data Bank [3], which houses over 130,000 biomolecular structures of protein and nucleic acids, open access enables scientists build on existing discoveries, which frees up resources for more impactful advancements. This can potentially translate to quicker scientific discoveries and treatments for incurable diseases such as cancer, HIV/AIDS and Alzheimer's disease.

At a time when issues surrounding research integrity and reproducibility are on the front burner, developing a transparent scientific culture and open approach to data sharing can uphold accountability and rigour. The role of social media in ushering this new era of open access cannot be understated. The Haruko Obokata STAP stem cell scandal in 2014 [4,5] immediately comes to mind—suspicions of scientific misconduct were initially discovered through discussions on two science blogs, Knoepfler Lab and PubPeer. Knowing that you have no monopoly of scientific truth and your datasets are open to public scrutiny will inspire a greater attention to detail and tame tendencies to overestimate research findings.

Increased public engagement is another incentive for a more inclusive research environment as it makes science more relevant to society. This is what citizen science hopes to achieve—by involving laypeople in scientific investigations, we can dispel negative stereotypes and increase public trust in science. It also encourages application of scientific thinking in everyday life and can inspire more people to pursue science careers. For 118 years, the Audubon Christmas Bird Count in the Americas has involved citizen scientists in collecting population data which have been used in conservation research and policy making [6] The project's remarkable longevity and success is a pointer to how widening public participation in research can extend the borders of scientific inquiry and drive reform. Recruiting the public for research activities has also proven to be labour-, time- and cost-effective, as seen with the FoldIt [7] and EyeWire [8,9] projects.

The past 20 years have witnessed tremendous changes in the global research landscape with respect to conduct of scientific inquiries, data sharing, engagement and publication. The gains notwithstanding, establishing an extensive and sustainable open research culture also requires addressing concerns over participant privacy, predatory publishing and protecting intellectual property. But if recent scientific advances are anything to go by, open research is here to stay.

References

1. Power, H. Predatory Publishing: How to Safely Navigate the Waters of Open Access. *Can. J. Nurs. Res.* **2018**, *50*, 3–8. [CrossRef] [PubMed]
2. McKiernan, E.C.; Bourne, P.E.; Brown, C.T.; Buck, S.; Kenall, A.; Lin, J.; McDougall, D.; Nosek, B.A.; Ram, K.; Soderberg, C.K.; et al. How Open Science Helps Researchers Succeed. *eLife* **2016**, *5*, e16800. [CrossRef] [PubMed]
3. Young, J.Y.; Westbrook, J.D.; Feng, Z.; Peisach, E.; Persikova, I.; Sala, R.; Sen, S.; Berrisford, J.M.; Swaminathan, G.J.; Oldfield, T.J. Worldwide Protein Data Bank biocuration supporting open access to high-quality 3D structural biology data. *Database*. 1 January 2018. Available online: https://doi.org/10.1093/database/bay002 (accessed on 10 October 2018).
4. Cyranoski, D. Stem-Cell Scientist Found Guilty of Misconduct. *Nature*. 1 April 2014. Available online: https://www.nature.com/news/stem-cell-scientist-found-guilty-of-misconduct-1.14974 (accessed on 10 October 2018).

5.   Rasko, J.; Power, C. What Pushes Scientists to Lie? The Disturbing But Familiar Story of Haruko Obota. *The Guardian*. 18 February 2015. Available online: https://www.theguardian.com/science/2015/feb/18/haruko-obokata-stap-cells-controversy-scientists-lie (accessed on 10 October 2018).

6.   Audubon. Available online: https://www.audubon.org/about/history-audubon-and-waterbird-conservation (accessed on 10 October 2018).

7.   FoldIt. Available online: https://fold.it/portal/info/about (accessed on 10 October 2018).

8.   Eyewire. Available online: https://eyewire.org/explore (accessed on 10 October 2018).

9.   EyeWire. A Game to Crowdsource Brain Mapping, 2016. CitizenScience. Available online: https://www.citizenscience.gov/eyewire-brain-mapping/# (accessed on 10 October 2018).

33 Open Research is a Blessing

Mai Sabry Saleh

Open research is a fast emerging concept in the last few decades that facilitates a vast scope of communication within the scientific community all over the world. Open access publishing, open data, open platforms, services and tools are terms increasing in popularity, and closely related to open research and collectively expressive about its ideology and practice. Open research also includes distance learning facilities like digital images, sound recordings, electronic libraries and published manuscripts.

By definition, open research is providing—within the scientific community—"transparency . . . through open access, open data, open communication and open source software" [1]. Hodgkinson-Williams and King define open research as a process in which research could be shared and freely accessed in the form of proposals, reviews, methodologies, analytical frameworks, findings and/or data . . . etc. "on an international scope under ethical practice and legal provenance" [2].

Open research is prevailing in the current era. Its vast spread is justified by the great impact it exerts on the advancement of research and excellence of researchers. Richness of available, transparent and reliable data from a broad variety of fields and disciplines is able to trigger innovative thinking and deeper understanding among researchers, which is prominently reflected in their scientific output [3].

Open access publishing, as one aspect highly linked with open research, is simply described as providing research with high visibility, accessibility and spread [4]. Open access publishing has provided good deal of publicity and encouraged academic usage with growing records in universal citation rates. In particular, the Gold Route open access—where open access journals publish scientific manuscripts freely online—offers authors a valuable chance of expressing their knowledge and transferring their experience. Moreover, open access publishing facilitates the precise process of peer-review and makes it easier to trace cited articles introduced as references within a manuscript under review. Besides this, it enhances the research process as a whole and among all categories of researchers, by facilitating access to literature in different fields of science, reducing time spent searching for data, increasing confidence of researchers in their work as they find it successfully published and repeatedly cited. In addition, it helps avoiding duplication of research work.

Open science is another evolutionary step in the field of scientific research. Open science makes science international. It offers the opportunity of collaborative projects, co-authorship and cross-border research opportunities. In fact, collaborative authorship has grown profoundly over the last thirty years. By definition, open science cares for enabling digital output of funded research to the scientific and public community. A key player in open science are tools for information and communication technologies (ICTs). Different online platforms can manage large data sets, publications and other kinds of project contents, and perfectly introduce them to those seeking them. Fortunately, ICTs have the potential capacity to turn science into being data-driven [5].

Open research has even made education available for everyone. Distance learning is mainly technology-mediated, where the teaching/learning process is implemented between individuals totally separated in time and space [6]. Globalization characteristics was one major trigger and participated—in addition to the rapid development of information technology—in providing a wide acceptance among users to learn electronically online. The predomination of the World Wide Web, and the affordable cost of processing and transmitting information has helped in the encouragement of such kinds of knowledge transfer [7]. Many that had lost hope in having appropriate opportunities for traditional ways of learning, found distance learning came to the rescue. Such groups include: women, working adults and those working with highly specialized materials and rare subjects. Developing countries lacking experts and pioneers in recent and up to date research methodologies and technicalities also appreciate being connected to the advanced research community through direct online contact. Distance learning has proved to be a persistent and permanent phenomenon, with increasing interest from a global population. It has been growing for fifteen years and is still in a continuous state of progress.

In their dreams, researchers never ask for more than what open research can provide them with. It is now a mere personal challenge for any true scientist to make his work visible, respected and figured out within the huge amounts of available of data and knowledge. Every researcher has the opportunity to prove himself and upgrade his abilities. It has become an equation gathering the two diverse concepts of individualism and collaboration for success and prominence. Open research, with its precious contribution to the scientific community, is a blessing that augments the chance for every person searching for his identity and eager for self-promotion to succeed and excel.

References

1. Ohmann, C.; Kuchinke, W. Future developments of medical informatics from the viewpoint of networked clinical research. *Methods Inf. Med.* **2009**, *48*, 45–54. [PubMed]
2. Hodgkinson-Williams, C.A.; King, T. Researching OER in the open: Developments in the ROER4D project. Unpublished Paper Underpinning Presentation at the 12th Annual Open Education Conference, Vancouver, BC, Canada, 18–20 November 2015; p. 5.
3. Johnson, H.J. Concordat on Open Research Data. 2016. Available online: http://www.rcuk.ac.uk/documents/documents/concordatonopenresearchdata-pdf/ (accessed on 21 August 2018).
4. Swan, A. #e Open Access Citation Advantage: Studies and Results to Date. 2010. Available online: http://eprints.ecs.soton.ac.uk/18516/ (accessed on 21 August 2018).
5. Force11. Improving the Future of Research Communications and e-Scholarship, Force11 White Paper, 2012. Available online: www.force11.org/white_paper (accessed on 21 August 2018).
6. Casarotti, M.; Filliponi, L.; Pieti, L.; Sartori, R. Educational interaction in distance learning: Analysis of one-way video and two-way audio system. *PsychNol. J.* **2002**, *1*, 28–38.
7. Webster, J.; Hackley, P. Teaching effectiveness in technology-mediated distance learning. *Acad. Manag. J.* **1997**, *40*, 1282–1309.

34   Prospects of Global Open Research

Auriol Degbelo

Type few keywords (say "privacy research articles") in a search engine of your choice (e.g., Google or Bing), and you will be overwhelmed by the number of results returned (typically in the order of hundreds of thousands). You start to browse through them by clicking on the links you see, and move from page to page. One of the links takes you straight to a PDF file which opens itself automatically. A smile appears on your face: you can skim through that article, apply Keshav's first pass of paper reading [1], and decide whether it is relevant or not. It happens to be relevant, and you store it without delay on your tablet. Job done! Encouraged by this success (after all, it only took 30 s to download the article and decide on its pertinence), you carry on with the next link. Though the title of this new article looks really cool, accessing the PDF this time seems less straightforward. You need to sign in to another system and pay a fee to be able to decide whether the article would be relevant or not. "Hmm. This article looks so great. The authors might have left a copy somewhere on their website", you say. You visit the authors' websites—still nothing. Meanwhile, two minutes are gone, not to say wasted. Yes, wasted. Because despite all your efforts, you're still at square one: you still don't know if that very nice article contains ideas worth re-using. You might perhaps never know, because by now you've given up (frustrated) and moved to the next link.

If you've tried at least once to collect scientific articles to complete a student assignment, prepare a lecture, write your own article, or simply feed your personal curiosity, you're certainly familiar with the experience described above. But there is great news! Open access to scientific articles is a trend that is gaining momentum. And this trend will save time: yours and ours. There was at least seven million researchers worldwide in 2013 according to the Unesco [2]. If each saved one minute per year not wasting time clicking on non-accessible articles (and this is a very generous assumption), this is seven million minutes saved per year worldwide and a gain of about 14 years—14 valuable years of human effort to reinvest in innovation and invention.

Scientific articles are one important product of research, but scholarly communication is shaped through many other artefacts. Indeed, the process of producing a research article involves the choice of a research method, the collection and subsequent analysis of research datasets, the development (or use) of tools, and the evaluation of the work done by one or more colleagues (also known as scholarly peer review). Open research intends to go beyond open access (i.e., PDF available for all) to make key artefacts used in scholarly communication—methods, datasets, tools, and peer-review discussions—openly accessible to everyone (Figure 1). I hope you begin to see what I see: if again each researcher saves one minute accessing any of these, this is a total of 70 years of human effort saved, a fantastic promise for open research!

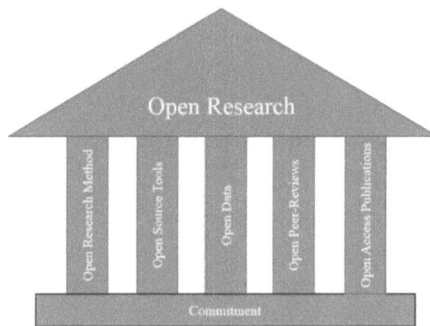

Figure 1. Open research rests on the commitment of people to make key artefacts of the research process freely accessible to everyone. It opens the door to substantial savings in human effort worldwide.

Knowledge accessible to all is a second key benefit of open research. For instance, buying one scientific article costs $15–30, and may be prohibitive to many. Figure 2 shows that there are at least two billion people worldwide living with less than $3.1 a day ($1132 annualized). These, clearly, may not afford using one percent of their annual income to access a single article. As said above, open research is more than open access to articles. It makes not only the final product of research (i.e., articles) free and available for anyone to re-use, but also the whole research factory (i.e., data, tools, methods, reviews) accessible to all. Open research thus lowers participation barriers to scientific discourse, enabling bright minds so far excluded to have their say and advance humanity's understanding of phenomena.

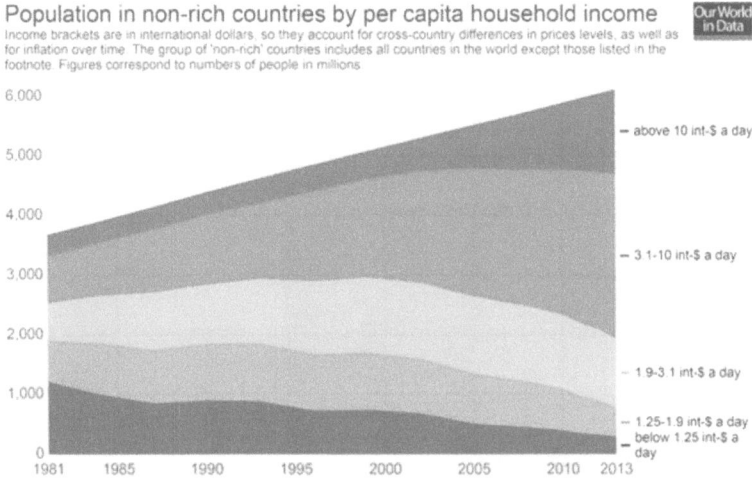

Figure 2. Population in non-rich countries by per capita household income [3]. Note: 'Non-rich' countries are all countries in the world except: Australia, Austria, Belgium, Canada, Cyprus, Denmark, Finland, France, Germany, Greece, Iceland, Ireland, Israel, Italy, Japan, Luxembourg, Netherlands, Norway, Portugal, Spain, Sweden, Switzerland, United Kingdom United States.

Besides substantial savings in time, and opening up new avenues for science through the inclusion of more people, open research holds the promise of enabling better research. First, the realization that the whole world can now see the inner workings of the research process is an incentive for researchers to engage in better documentation [4], and research methods. Next, making research artefacts open prevents reinventing the wheel, because it helps get a better impression of what has been achieved, and channel resources to truly unsolved problems. Last, open research paves the way for follow-up studies, which verify the conclusions of scientific analyses. Henderson [5] provided a compelling example of the pertinence of these follow-up studies in science. A picture of a piece of rock on Mars in 1976 created the illusion of a human face (see Figure 3), and opened the door to much speculation. The picture of the same piece of rock in 2001—from a different angle and at a better resolution—revealed that the "face" was not a face at all. So we need follow-up studies to confirm or infirm our conclusions in science. And being transparent about artefacts of the whole research process provides a baseline against which these follow-up studies can compare against.

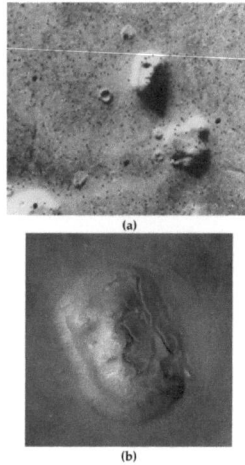

Figure 3. Pictures of a piece of rock on Mars in 1976 **(a)** and 2001 **(b)** [6].

References

1. Keshav, S. How to read a paper. *ACM SIGCOMM Comput. Commun. Rev.* **2007**, *37*, 83–84. [CrossRef]
2. UNESCO. Facts and Figures from the UNESCO Science Report. Available online: https://en.unesco.org/unesco_science_report/figures (accessed on 20 February 2018).
3. Roser, M.; Ortiz-Ospina, E. Global Extreme Poverty, 2018. Our World in Data. Available online: https://ourworldindata.org/extreme-poverty (accessed on 31 August 2018).
4. Tennant, J.P.; Waldner, F.; Jacques, D.C.; Masuzzo, P.; Collister, L.B.; Hartgerink, C.H.J. The academic, economic and societal impacts of Open Access: An evidence-based review. *F1000Research* **2016**, *5*, 632. [CrossRef] [PubMed]
5. Dakin Henderson. Why Should Scientific Results Be Reproducible? Available online: http://www.pbs.org/wgbh/nova/next/body/reproducibility-explainer/ (accessed on 27 February 2018).
6. NASA. Unmasking the Face on Mars, 2001. NASA Science. Available online: https://science.nasa.gov/science-news/science-at-nasa/2001/ast24may_1 (accessed on 31 August 2018).

35 Open Access: a Two-Way Path for the Underprivileged

Stefania Noerman

Most people around the globe live in underprivileged areas. In the world of science, this would mean that most global citizens have limited access to the literature and do not get updates to the latest research in the field. The paywalls to scientific journals restrict the amount of information because the subscription fees cost a lot of money. In these areas, the same amount can be used to hire a technical assistant or buy laboratory supplies, which are more fundamental to perform research. Though I do not mean that literature or the latest scientific articles in the field are negligible, obtaining a paid article is not entirely impossible. Talking from personal experience, when I get stuck at a paywall for an article which, after reading the abstract, would be essential for my research, I can ask my colleagues in some other institutes to download the full-text article. Of course, I cannot do it too often or for too many materials, due to my conscience.

We, as scientists, completely realize how crucial it is to publish our research article in a freely accessible journal. I believe that all of us have had the devastating experience of requiring a paid report, and how we like the feeling of getting all the articles we need. On the other hand, publishing in the free-access journals can cost quite a lot. Not to mention the public who may not include the journal subscription in their budget. Academic or research institutes need to carefully consider how they will spend the annual budget and make hard choices on several journals' subscriptions. Hence, open science may provide a solution to cater to the hunger of the scientific community and public society for highly-qualified research articles.

In the university where I am doing my doctoral studies now, we are encouraged to do open research. One of the reasons is to transparently give a freely-accessible research output to funding bodies and the public society. There are several options for how we can do that. As the first option, as much as we can, we should publish our research articles in a freely accessible journal. The idea behind open access journals is to divert the publication cost from readers to authors. Because the journals will not charge the readers, the costs to keep the journal running are then covered by the authors. Because the numbers of authors will most likely be less than the readers, the reviewing and publication fee can be high. I do not mean that publication in the free journals is more expensive than with publishers with a paywall, but the researchers need to take this cost into consideration. Unless the researchers have included the publication fee in the grant application proposal, the budget limitation will restrict the options of journals available for selection. In that sense, researchers stuck between the necessities of the latest research update in the field and the institutes who cannot afford to pay all the publishers in the world need to contemplate how to get the best balance between the pricing factors and other scientifically favorable factors.

I like the idea of a second scenario to make this open science an answer to the desperate need of scientific field, without sacrificing the necessities of our host institutions. Regardless of whatever journals the researchers pick, they can self-archive the freely accessible version somewhere else. For this purpose, we can use the service of the university library, because the librarians have expertise in this area. Another exciting way to do it is by utilization of social media. With the flourishing usage of social media, including in the scientific community, authors can upload the accepted authors' manuscript, before the publisher's editing takes place, in their social media accounts after the embargo period.

Using such social media as a "free" means of open science, one scientist can network with the others both in similar or different areas. Due to the nature of social media itself, we can enlarge the networking scope from those we know or have met to those we did not have any connection to before. This network nonetheless will be valuable to foster future research collaborations with limitless possibilities of inter-disciplinary partnership one can expect. As all scientists aim for ground-breaking research, a sophisticated study employing multiple approaches and hence expertise in different fields is a challenge we would like to embrace. Thus, open science may also accelerate the generation of research itself, improve quality of a study, increase the number of publications, and hence enable faster completion of the research cycle than ever before.

For the stakeholders, such as the funding bodies, governments, or other regulatory organizations, easily accessible research provides them with more information for their decision-making processes. The funding bodies, who have supported the study would like to know how the support has been implemented to advance scientific discovery and benefit society. This information may also lay some foundation for the future studies they would like to support, aligned with their aims. At the same time, research outputs may also trigger governmental or other regulatory organizations to modify some regulations or to create the new ones that may solve some problems or benefit the public.

With all the excitement surrounding the idea of open science, the full implementation may take some time because not all of us are familiar with the related processes. Hence, witnessing the expected benefits would take even longer time, especially in fostering research collaborations. The public domain will firstly be showered with the overwhelming amount of information, which will hopefully sharpen critical thinking to assess and select which one they want to believe and apply in their daily life. In the less developed parts of the world, this challenge will hopefully change the delivery system of public education, which may also stimulate the progression of science and its application to ease their burden. In the end, all of us need science for a better life, right?

36 Open Research: Interlinking Sanctuaries of Knowledge

James Guo Sheng Moo

Science research has been a backbone of innovation driven economies. The unique ideas and information created have been used in products that change human lives for the better. That said, entering the 21st century, the scientific scene has witnessed several developments, including interconnectivity between nations, information boom from the internet scape and the growing use of crowd sourcing. Inevitably, it has altered the career opportunities that are presented to scientists. Open access to research also provides a window of opportunity for the next leap in technology development.

Traditionally, the rite of passage for a scientist includes entering the graduate school, expanding his or her scope by doing post-doctoral fellowships with professors before entering the faculty or joining the research arm of a company. All these are accomplished by publishing subscription-based journal articles, which are often very costly. This limits access from developing nations, which often do not have the resources to obtain these trinkets of knowledge. At the same time, are we truly limited to being examined by our hard skills and technical expertise that we have developed? I believe that the creativity and analytical skills that we have honed play an even more critical role. In addition, our training often emphasises the technicalities and sometimes overlook the fact that the greatest idea must be communicated to the masses and to let the public understand the potential reaping that we can harvest. This is where open research can come in to allow for the next generation of scientists to benefit from a time of global exchange of ideas.

The next generation of scientists need to transmit the information he or she developed to the masses. Being a communicator, the scientist will possess soft skills in order to relate these topics to the public and the corporate world. Open research provides a tool for these ideas to be communicated freely across channels. These characteristics are also needed in a team, involving personnel from different fields. Modern research requires inputs from diverse fields and much co-operation. A collaborative approach from the scientist allow further exploration into the subject, where a critical mass from different approaches can be reached. This correlates with the fact that modern research takes an interdisciplinary approach. Having the above traits, also endow the scientist transferable skills that can be widely applied across differing arenas.

Mobility of these scientific ideas cannot be more accentuated. In the age of innovation-driven economies, talents move from countries to countries and are highly mobile. The equal can be said of ideas, where open and unfettered access should be allowed. The knowledge capital that is generated is largely dependent on the people. A team of creative scientists can translate ideas into realities. This is in addition to the recent trend of internet-led crowd-funding, where funds can be raised and information and facilities are shared remotely through sharing of information. Access to these resources and intellectual properties liberates the scientists from any limitations. Thus, a scientist's work is now unconfined. Open access allows us to build bridges instead of walls and to allow unhindered access to knowledge and information, being key to build on the work of forerunners.

Globalisation has eliminated barriers and the internet has hastened information exchange. Free-flowing ideas now pulsate through the optical fibres from one end of the world to the other. This has accelerated the interplay of ideas, allowing the best ones to emerge. It has also become critically important to discern true knowledge from a plethora of data. Ideas are of economic value, as they translate eventually into intellectual property as patents and then as products. What does it mean for us as scientists then? An innovation-driven economy means for us that more people from universities can partake and engage the global community through open access portals. In the private sector, researchers can also rapidly adopt these new technologies for products and doctorate-holding consultants authenticate new patents.

Thus said, translation of ideas have also started at the academia, where spinoffs prototype them into industrial products. The public-private partnerships have spawned a need for intermediaries to explain technical know-how to the corporate world. This means that the labor market's hunger for scientific talents is huge, albeit one that requires these scientists to be able to communicate the information to the masses and one who has transferrable skills that can work in the corporate world. Co-operation from federal bodies is also needed for this to take place. This continued commitment of governments and their recognition that scientific works and ideas are altruistic, generates economic growth, will continue to lead the investment in education and science. Open access to information will allow sanctuaries of knowledge to interlink and build a network of possibilities to accelerate the next leap in technology development. In next the step towards a sharing economy, where benefits of technological developments should trickle to every strata of the society, ideas should be shared and not confined.

MDPI

St. Alban-Anlage 66

4052 Basel

Switzerland

Tel. +41 61 683 77 34

Fax +41 61 302 89 18

www.mdpi.com

MDPI Books Editorial Office

E-mail: books@mdpi.com

www.mdpi.com/books

MDPI

www.ingramcontent.com/pod-product-compliance
Lightning Source LLC
Chambersburg PA
CBHW041242020426

42333CB00003B/52